NOTES ON MOZART

NOTES ON MOZART

20 Crucial Works

Conrad Wilson

William B. Eerdmans Publishing Company
Grand Rapids, Michigan

For Cosima and Marcella

First published 2003 by Saint Andrew Press, Edinburgh

This edition published 2005
in the United States of America by
Wm. B. Eerdmans Publishing Company
255 Jefferson Ave. S.E., Grand Rapids, Michigan 49503

Printed in the United States of America

10 09 08 07 06 05   7 6 5 4 3 2 1

ISBN 0–8028–2929–5

www.eerdmans.com

CONTENTS

gratis

v

FOREWORD

Why twenty? Obviously it is a device, one way of drawing attention to some of the masterpieces in a great composer's output. But at the same time it is a discipline and a challenge. Why choose these particular works and not others? The question and its answers are my reason for writing this book and its companions on other composers. In making my selection, I thought twenty works to be a good, sufficiently tight number. Increase it to thirty and choice becomes easier, perhaps too easy. Reduce it to ten and, in the case of great productive composers, you don't really have enough music wholly to justify what you are doing. Too many crucial works would have to be excluded, and the gaps would be glaring. So twenty it is, though not in the sense of a top twenty, because a crucial work does not actually have to be a great one, and the works are not listed – how could they be? – in any order of merit.

But each of them, it seems to me, needs to mark a special moment in its composer's life – perhaps a turning point, perhaps a sudden flash of inspiration, perhaps an intensifying of genius, as when Schubert produced his setting of Goethe's 'Gretchen am Spinnrade' at the age of 17, or Mozart his G major Violin Concerto, K216, at 19, or Beethoven his C minor Piano Trio, Op. 1, No. 3, at 25.

None of these composers was a prodigy as gifted as Mendelssohn, whose String Octet and whose *A Midsummer Night's Dream* overture were the most astounding teenage masterpieces of all time. But if there was nothing so arresting to be found among Mozart's or Schubert's numerous boyhood works, the change when it came was startling.

With Schubert's first great song, Mozart's first great concerto and Beethoven's first great piece of chamber music came the shock of surprise in the form of an audacious new command of melody and accompaniment, a conspicuous leap in quality and, in the slow movement of the Mozart, a grasp of the mystery of beauty which made his two previous violin concertos, written in the same year, seem blandly impersonal exercises in composition.

Yet this third of Mozart's five violin concertos is not a masterpiece in the sense that *Don Giovanni* is, just as Schubert's boyhood String Quartet in E flat major, D87, for all its melodic beauty, is not as overwhelming as 'Death and the Maiden'. Nor, for that matter, does Beethoven's Second Symphony possess the size and sustaining power of his Third, the 'Eroica', though it has unquestionable excitements of its own.

It is not the aim of these books to set one masterpiece against another, or to suggest that early works are automatically less interesting than late ones. To regard a composer's output purely as a process of evolution is to fail inexcusably to accept a work on its own terms — a serious flaw in assessments of Schubert, who, according to many a pundit, did not 'find' himself until he was almost dead.

So, early works are not being banned from these pages, even if it means the loss of some late ones. Nor is my decision to deal with the music chronologically based on any intrinsic belief that it reflects in some special way a composer's progress. The intention is simply to shed light on what was happening to him at the time he wrote a particular piece, where he was, what he was doing or experiencing, and how the music fits into the general pattern of his life and output. To go beyond this, by claiming that Haydn, for example, 'progressed' from his *Storm and Stress* symphonies to his *London* ones, or Mozart from his E flat major Piano Concerto, K271, to his E flat major, K482, is to undervalue his achievement as a whole.

So, no masterpiece has been omitted simply because its composer later in some way surpassed it. Some works are included simply because I adore them, or am prepared to defend them against the judgement of people who detest them. Liking a piece of music, we should always remember, is not the opposite of disliking it. It is a different condition altogether, and being able to explain why we like it is perhaps more important in the end than pronouncing on whether it is good music or bad.

Each of these twenty short essays is a species of what are traditionally known as programme notes — the descriptions to be found in printed concert or opera programmes of what is being performed that night. Donald Francis Tovey, one-time professor of music at Edinburgh University, was a famed and erudite pioneer of the form in the early twentieth century, and his collected *Essays in Musical Analysis* remain good to read, even if their style now seems old-fashioned and out of tune with today's musical thinking. Nor are they always accurate. Scholarship has progressed since Tovey's time.

Nevertheless, what Tovey wrote still towers over much of what passes for programme notes today. Even during my own post-Tovey boyhood, programme notes incorporated – as Tovey's did – musical examples because it was assumed that concert-goers could read music. Today, such notes would be branded elitist. To include musical terminology at all tends to be frowned upon. I have been asked why, in my own notes, I employ such terms as 'counterpoint', which nobody understands. But are football correspondents similarly chided for writing 'penalty' or 'free kick'? Somehow I think not. Though I am all against jargon, the use of an established, accessible musical term is preferable to a paragraph of explanation.

Concert programmes are now a dumbed-down art in which fatuous puffs about the performers occupy more space than the notes themselves, and adverts are given more space still. Traditional notes, as the chief executive of a concert organisation has remarked to me, are now 'irrelevant'. In the sense that most concerts today take place in darkened halls, he was perhaps right. But notes are written to be read before and after an event, as well as during it, and this book's intention is to fill that need.

In the sixteen years I spent editing the Edinburgh Festival's programme notes, there were a number of house rules which I worked out with the then Festival director, Peter Diamand, whose European outlook differed from, and was refreshingly less 'commercial' than, the British. Diamand's beliefs, which I shared, were that notes should contain facts rather than flimflam; that speculation was acceptable so long as it was informed; that notes should be coherently devised by a single writer for the contents of a single programme; that connections between one work and another should be mentioned; that the author, as Tovey once decreed, should act as counsel for the defence – Diamand detested notes which gave the impression that 'This is a bad work but let's perform it anyway'; and that artists' biographies should be confined to 150 words, should include no adjectives and should supply no information about what a performer would be performing in future seasons.

Though most of these principles have fallen by the wayside, they are still the ones to which I, as a note-writer, would prefer to adhere. In addition, I would say that, wherever possible, a work's place in musical history needs to be established; that its local connections (if any) should be mentioned; and that the writer has a responsibility to lure the reader into the music.

Some of the notes included in these pages are based on notes originally written for one musical organisation or another, but which have gone through a constant process of change, and which have now been changed yet again to suit the needs of a book about a single great composer. No note, whether for a concert programme or for something more permanent, should be merely 'drawn from stock'. Just as every performance of a work forms a part (however small) of that work's history, so every programme note should reflect the state – and status – of that work at the time the annotator is writing about it. Attitudes alter. Here, in this book, are twenty current attitudes (my own, but also quoting those of others) to twenty works that continue to matter.

Finally, a note on format. Each book begins with a fresh assessment of its subject composer and of the way he is performed at the start of the twenty-first century. Books are listed for further reading, and technical terms are explained in a brief glossary. Recordings are recommended at the end of each short essay, with record numbers provided wherever possible. Since prices vary from shop to shop, it seems sensible simply to generalise, saying where a disc, or set of discs, is bargain-price or otherwise at the time of going to press.

CONRAD WILSON
Edinburgh, 2003

INTRODUCTION

Mozart, a composer long seen through a distorting lens, is at last coming into something like accurate focus. Though it has taken more than two centuries to sift the facts from the fictions, we now know enough about this seemingly most familiar, yet in many ways most elusive, of geniuses to be able to relate the man to the music. No longer are we so eager to accept myth, assumption and guesswork in place of firm evidence about him. What we want, as Pamina so eloquently cries in Act One of *The Magic Flute*, is 'The Truth'.

Was he really a wunderkind, the most wondrous of them all? Did he love his wife or prefer her sister? Was he as impoverished and misunderstood as he has been made out to be? Was his father a good or a bad influence on him? Are his letters to be trusted? Did he or did he not like the flute as an instrument? How did he die? Do we tend to read more into his music than is really there? Even now, not all these questions can be answered to complete satisfaction. There remain glaring gaps in our knowledge of him. And, though his correspondence with his father is a primary source of valuable information, it tantalisingly grinds to a halt after Leopold's death in 1787, at a crucial moment in the composer's creative and personal life. Too much still rests in the realms of speculation.

As recently as 1982, Wolfgang Hildesheimer, one of the more abrasive and radical of Mozart's recent biographers, felt obliged to correct many still extant beliefs about him. Launching his book with an assault on some of the waffle produced by supposedly reliable authorities, he made you wonder how it could have been swallowed for so long. It was, after all, a question not simply of facts but also of attitudes. The observation of the influential and distinguished musical biographer Alfred Einstein, that Mozart 'was only a guest on this earth', was maybe acceptable as an emotional statement, declared Hildesheimer, though only on an 'uncomfortably irrational level'. He omitted to add, however, that it was a level no higher than Grillparzer's deplorable Schubert epitaph – 'a rich treasure but still fairer hopes' – with its demeaning implication of promise unfulfilled.

But Mozart, like Schubert, has always been subject to such tributes, whether they have come from the theologian Karl Barth, who claimed that the angels, left to themselves, performed Mozart, or from the publisher Nikolaus Simrock, who doffed his hat whenever Mozart's name was mentioned. Today the worst of the Mozart mystique may be dead, but it has yet to be laid to rest.

As a result, Peter Shaffer in *Amadeus* had no trouble reviving the old misconception that Mozart may have been killed by his supposedly jealous Viennese rival, Antonio Salieri, though the play in other respects had interesting things to say about the nature of genius. Its suggestion that Salieri, a more devout man than Mozart, was upset because it was his insufferably foul-mouthed young rival upon whom God bestowed genius, rather than upon the more deserving Salieri himself, was one way of pointing out that great composers are not always nice people. Had Shaffer chosen Wagner, a more obvious subject for such a play, the point would have been lost. It had to be the divine and untainted Mozart who was shown to be imperfect. The fact that Salieri, in reality, shouted his enthusiasm after every number in *The Magic Flute* was beside the point.

All three of these composers, in fact, had good conceits of themselves, though Mozart's vanity, fanned by his father, too easily landed him in trouble. The Empress Maria Theresa was not the only aristocratic figure to display her contempt for the cocky young musical upstart when she wrote to her influential son telling him not to waste his time on Salzburg 'riffraff' such as the Mozarts, nor to employ them in Milan, where the 15-year-old composer wrote one of the biggest and most imposing of his early operas, *Mitridate*, as well as the exquisite and much-loved little motet, *Exsultate Jubilate*.

Yet Mozart got his revenge on his social superiors in two operatic master-pieces, *Figaro's Wedding* and *Don Giovanni*, and did it in a way that did not deprive him of an audience. By 1786, when *Figaro* hit the Viennese stage, his reputation as an opera-composer was established, even though people found some of his music 'difficult'. By 1791, just before his death, *The Magic Flute* widened his public and endeared him to everybody, even if he died too soon to appreciate fully what he had achieved.

He was fully aware, however, of his creative self-reliance and single-minded genius. Nobody but Mozart could have produced something as class-consciously audacious as the 'three-orchestra trick' at the end of Act One of *Don Giovanni*, where three different ensembles simultaneously play three interlocking dances for the three clearly differentiated social classes represented at Giovanni's ball. He knew his own worth, and was better paid for it than posterity has been prepared to believe. Mozart's money problems derived more from reckless spending than from a pauper's income. Indeed, the communal grave into which his body was lowered in December 1791 carried no social stigma for which Vienna could be posthumously blamed. It was simply the form of burial – hygienic and space-saving – recommended at the time by the emperor and encouraged by the city's authorities. The politically left-wing and philosophically enlightened Mozart, even in death, was nothing if not progressive.

Had he survived his final fever, which was of a sort he had suffered at least once before, what might he have produced or done? As the pianist Alfred Brendel has admitted in a recent book, Mozart's death is the one he finds hardest to forgive. Yet he did not display genius from the start. His childhood minuets were all very well; but Mendelssohn by the mature age of 16 was a better composer. His String Octet and *A Midsummer Night's Dream* overture were more miraculous, if such a word is permissible, than anything Mozart had written at a similar age. On the other hand, it was Mozart who learned how to develop his genius, producing in his later years masterpieces unfathomable in their greatness and imaginative invention, with a fecundity confirmed by the 600-plus works listed in Kochel's Mozart catalogue.

Yet Mozart the gifted boy, the charming, precocious, cherubic child, devotedly cultivated in his native Salzburg, remains a tourist attraction who will never be allowed to die. His early keyboard pieces, tinkling out of kitschy music boxes, and his portraits not quite meeting your eye from the lids of chocolate boxes in shop windows, continue to mar your pleasure in what is otherwise still a beautiful if sometimes chilling city. But in the end the music, the real music, is what counts, and we are now closer to what it is about than we have ever been before.

A performance by a high-quality specialist ensemble, by the French-based Quatuor Mosaïques or the English Baroque Soloists, has a keenly defined truthfulness we can sense, even while still coming to terms with our realisation that this is how it should really sound. It is not the Mozart of the well-upholstered Vienna Philharmonic, or of the conductor Bruno Walter, who liked to slow up for the expressive second themes in the opening movements of Mozart's symphonies, and who condescendingly described Mozart as 'an open, trusting soul'. Nor is it the glowing but complacent Mozart of Karl Boehm, or the suavely cold-hearted Mozart of Herbert von Karajan, whose recording of the Symphony No. 29 is surely unique in that, when you listen to it as an entity, every tempo sounds wrong. Today, we have got beyond all that and have come to recognise — which is greatly to Mozart's benefit — that some of the best performances of his music take place beyond Austria.

Johann Chrysostom Wolfgang Amadeus Mozart was born in Salzburg on 27 January 1756. He was the last of Leopold Mozart's seven children, only two of whom survived. The other, four years older, was Maria Anna, known as 'Nannerl'. She became a talented pianist. He became a child prodigy, toured round Europe by his ambitious, attentive, pedagogic father. A musician himself – composer of what used to be known as Haydn's Toy Symphony, *a good violinist, and author of an important book on that instrument – Leopold was nobody's fool. He presided scrupulously over Wolfgang's development as a composer, which began at the age of 5 with a pair of keyboard pieces in which Leopold himself surely had a hand.*

His relationship with Wolfgang was musically strong, largely loving, but ultimately – with Nannerl receiving more of his attention – less close. His promotion of himself and his son as a musical 'package' had not always been in Wolfgang's best interests, and may have lost him some beneficial jobs when possible employers realised that in order to get the son they also had to accept the father. But Leopold, at least, kept a stern eye on money. It was in Vienna, away from his father's close attention, and with a wife and family on his hands, that Wolfgang's finances became a problem.

One

1775
VIOLIN CONCERTO NO. 3 IN G MAJOR, K216

Allegro   Adagio   Rondeau: Allegro

At the age of 19, Mozart composed five violin concertos, between the first and last of which the child prodigy suddenly grew into an adult. The pivotal concerto was the third, K216 in G major, and many romantic words have been devoted to speculating on how – after two pleasing but thoroughly perfunctory works – he struck gold. All five concertos, after all, were written within the space of a few months, the first two in the spring of 1775, the others in the autumn and winter. What created the 'enormous and incomprehensible gulf', as a distinguished Mozart authority has accurately put it, which exists between the impersonality of the D major concerto, K211, and the genius of its successor in G major?

Perhaps it was melodic inspiration, conspicuously absent from the previous concertos. Perhaps it was the potent discovery that his new melodic gift was of a wonderfully vocal, indeed positively operatic, nature, with the violin as the voice. Perhaps it was a stronger and more personal grasp of the possibilities of his basic material, and an ability to employ it to more passionate purpose. Already that year, he had finished his operatic comedy, *La finta giardiniera*, and his pastoral music drama, *Il re pastore*, overtones of which pervade K216. Indeed, *Il re pastore* contains an inspired soprano aria with solo violin obbligato which shows quite clearly where the roots of the G major concerto lay.

So, in saluting the sudden greatness of this work, we should also admit that its predecessors, which soloists continue to perform because they are by Mozart, were conspicuously characterless. We should also admit that, after this great leap forwards, there were innumerable leaps backwards into musical blandness. Mozart at 19 was not yet the consistently great composer he was to become. To put in a similar claim on behalf of the so-called 'Jeunehomme' Piano Concerto in E flat major, K271, as Alfred Brendel has done, would be equally easy. As a pianist, Brendel can show how it towers over its predecessors and compares with its successors. But the violin concertos K216, 218 and 219 came first.

The quality of these works speaks for itself. They are not only prodigiously inspired but also fascinatingly contrasted in a variety of ways. Not even the great Mozart specialist, H. C. Robbins Landon, can tell us exactly why he wrote them, though we can guess that it was primarily to please his father, an outstanding violinist and violin teacher who wanted his son to surpass him. In fact, the teenage Wolfgang – who had taught himself the violin at the age of 7 – already believed he had done so. Writing home from a trip to Munich, he spoke of how he had played the solo part in one of his divertimentos 'as though I were the greatest violinist in all of Europe'.

So we can assume that he composed his violin concertos for himself to perform in his role as Konzertmeister of the Salzburg Court Orchestra. Then, having written them and achieved perfection in them, he found piano concertos more to his taste. Once he had moved to Vienna, and left his father behind in Salzburg, he produced no more violin concertos and concentrated instead on being Europe's greatest pianist, a position he held until Beethoven took over from him.

Yet the three great violin works – and their inspired spin-off in the form of the Sinfonia Concertante for violin and viola, K364, written four years later – hold a special place in his output, and the G major remains a particularly sophisticated example of his youthful genius. It is brilliantly alive to all the trends of the time, to the French school of violin music as well as the Italian and Austrian. Of all these he had gained first-hand experience in his travels as a prodigy, with his father as chaperon. Its finale, for instance, is entitled *rondeau* (French) rather than 'rondo' (standard German and Italian usage), and in tribute to its French name it incorporates an unexpected gavotte-like interlude. The first movement of K216 provides more subtle repartee between soloist and orchestra, complete with the arrival of a brand-new theme in the middle, than does any other Mozart concerto up to that time. In the adagio, a magical change of colour takes place through the unexpected substitution of flutes for oboes (implying that Mozart's Salzburg oboists were also flautists). The soft throb of muted strings beneath the soloist's songlike main theme here gives the music a serene, dreamlike quality prophetic of the slow movement of the great C major Piano Concerto, K467, so poetically used in the film *Elvira Madigan*.

The flow of the finale is somewhat different, its swinging main theme meeting various obstacles – changes of tempo, rhythm and mood – all of them deftly surmounted. The gavotte episode in G minor, with its trills and pizzicati, provides a mysterious foretaste of the dance music in Act Three of *Figaro's Wedding*. G minor would later become known as Mozart's darkest key; even in this convivial movement, it casts a shadow across the music. The more robust section which follows is believed to have been based, with what sounds like private Mozart hilarity, on a folk tune known as the *Strassburger*, which may have been familiar to the original audience.

Though most of today's great violinists have recorded Mozart's concertos, too many of them have skated across the surface of the music, fiddling sweetly and narcissistically but never getting to grips with what the concertos are about. Beauty of tone is not enough, though it is about all we get from Henryk Szeryng, Itzhak Perlman, Yehudi Menuhin, Isaac Stern, Pinchas Zukerman and others, especially if they are teamed with weighty accompanists such as Herbert von Karajan or Wolfgang Sawallisch.

Arthur Grumiaux comes nearer the mark; but the crispest, most stylish, least cloying, most fizzing performance of K216 is one of the most recent

– the Russian Viktoria Mulanova's with the beautifully scaled Orchestra of the Age of Enlightenment (Philips 470 292-2). With vivacious cadenzas, and bright, light-toned Mozartian sonorities, the disc also includes the witty K218 in D major and (an enlightening comparison) K207 in B flat major, which not even Mulanova can bring to life.

After completing his sequence of violin concertos, but before recognising that his future lay in the piano, Mozart dallied with the idea of composing concertos for more than one instrument. It was, on the whole, a bad idea. A double concerto for piano and violin was begun but abandoned. So was a more ambitious work for violin, viola and cello. A charming concerto for flute and harp did get written, and remains popular, though it was rather too dainty to be worthy of his name. A concerto for two pianos proved wittier and more robust, without being the masterpiece he was groping towards.

A disguised violin concerto, no masterpiece either, was infiltrated into the framework of the genial but rambling 'Haffner' serenade, a bundle of wedding pieces written for the Salzburg family whose name would be further immortalised by his more impressive 'Haffner' symphony a little later. These works, among the last products of his Salzburg youth, show that he was ready for escape — but to where?

A journey to Paris, with his mother as chaperon, ended with her death and a rebuke from his father for not looking after her properly. The musically industrious city of Mannheim, by then past its prime, offered scraps of opportunity. Munich, just along the road from Salzburg, beckoned more strongly, and gave him the chance to compose Idomeneo, *his first great opera, for what was now the finest opera company in Europe. In the end, however, it was Vienna that got him, even if it was insufficiently aware of its good luck.*

Two

1779
SINFONIA CONCERTANTE IN E FLAT MAJOR FOR VIOLIN, VIOLA AND ORCHESTRA, K364

Allegro maestoso   Andante   Presto

Amid all the frustrations of what turned out to be his last days in Salzburg, Mozart produced this grandly passionate work for violin, viola and orchestra. Nobody knows why he did so, or for whom he wrote it. But one thing is clear. As a bright young composer of concertos, he had been searching for fresh ideas, and, after a series of botched shots, this was where he found them. It is a work which stands in isolation, even its name seeming to set it apart from the rest of his output. But, in choosing to call it a sinfonia concertante, or 'symphony with concerto elements', he was making a point. The difference was more than a matter of semantics. The music is not at all like the concerto for two pianos which holds the adjacent Kochel number.

Eric Blom, in his now obsolescent *Master Musician* study of the composer, was right to admire its beautiful dark colouring – 'not at all suited', as he observed, 'to the archiepiscopal court, and perhaps disclosing active revolt against it'. Though this was wisdom after the event, the music shows exactly why Archbishop Hieronymus Colloredo of Salzburg was accusing Mozart of neglecting his ecclesiastical duties. Not only was he playing the organ half-heartedly in Salzburg Cathedral, but he was composing irrelevant, perhaps even subversively passionate works such as this sinfonia concertante.

Whether or not the archbishop ever heard it – and, as Leopold Mozart complained, court concerts became restricted in length during Colloredo's reign – the sinfonia concertante was hardly a work to set his mind at rest. Whereas in the concerto for two pianos everything lay sparklingly on the surface, in the sinfonia concertante for two string players a great deal went on below. As its title implied, Mozart was at pains to integrate the soloists more closely with the rest of the orchestra.

In such a work, there would in any case have been a natural tendency to do so. Solo string tone is tailored more easily to the sound of orchestral strings than piano tone. Yet Mozart does seem to have gone out of his way here to obtain a deliberately 'symphonic' richness of texture by dividing the orchestral violas into two separate groups, thus giving the music an extra tenor line which deepens the sonority in the same way as his use of two violas in his great series of string quintets would do later.

But the music is more than a matter of contrasts between violin and viola tone, even though that is unquestionably one of its arresting features. Here, as in no comparable work of its period, the listener is enabled to appreciate the not invariably obvious difference between the sound of the violin playing at the bottom of its register and the viola playing at the top.

Plainly, these were aspects of the sinfonia which fascinated Mozart, who was an adept performer on both instruments, and who in the first performance probably played the viola, as increasingly became his custom in works with a solo viola part. Often here, the instruments become two characters in a drama. There are times when the violin is shadowed by the viola, a few bars behind. There are times when Mozart employs melodic phrases that can turn in two different directions or explore two different moods.

Ambiguity was always a feature of his music, and here he employed it to create a deliberate sense of unrest, as in the powerful symphonic sweep of the opening material. The broad, majestic flow of the main theme never quite conceals the feelings that simmer below its elegant surface. Little interjections from oboes and horns get swept aside by a big orchestral crescendo in which Mozart seems deliberately to be showing the Mannheim symphonists (who were specialists in crescendos) that he could beat them at their own game.

Though textures are beautifully balanced, Mozart took no chances over the solo viola part. To ensure that this sometimes reticent instrument would be fully audible, he scored its music in the key of D major, not E flat major, thus requiring the player to tune a semitone sharp in order to produce the keener-edged tone required. It was an old Austrian ploy, known as *scordatura*, which had been developed a century earlier by H. J. Biber, and would be revived by Mahler, for reasons of his own, in the scherzo of his Fourth Symphony. Today's big-toned viola players generally see no need to go through what they regard as an unnecessary retuning process, though in an 'authentic' performance of the work on period instruments they would continue to do so.

But if the first movement has its emotional ambiguities, there is no ambiguity whatever about the technical demands it places on the soloists. It is very difficult to play, as is confirmed by the quantity of maladroit performances it still receives. Not only is it one of Mozart's largest-scale opening movements, with a rich diversity of themes, but it provides very little respite for either of the soloists, one or other of whom is constantly being required to make eloquent statements that demand equally eloquent answers. The magnificent and challenging cadenza for the two instruments is Mozart's own.

About the central andante there is no ambiguity of any sort. This is one of the saddest of all Mozart's slow movements, a long lament in C minor, quite operatic in its singing lines, the violin tone often sounding as veiled and viola-like as that of the viola itself. Though G minor was famously Mozart's most personal and poignant key, C minor, as here, was its frequent rival. The 23-year-old Mozart's ability to pour his heart out in one troubled phrase after another is the movement's most memorable feature – so much so that, when the witty finale is at last unleashed, its raciness comes as a shock. Yet its effect is never trivial. Rather, it acts like the closing of a door on things that have been too hard to bear. Its resourcefully jovial progress is a delight, though for the soloists there is no relaxation. Moreover, they must hold enough power in reserve to hit their respective top E flats which Mozart operatically demands from them towards the end.

The shortage of good recordings of this sinfonia concertante should come as no surprise. To get at the fine performance by Arthur Grumiaux and Arrigo Pellicia, you have to buy the five violin concertos as well, though at least the two-disc set sells at a bargain price (Philips Duo 438 323-2). The father-and-son team of David and Igor Oistrakh is to be avoided (too perfunctory); but the reissue of an old Cleveland Orchestra performance, dating from George Szell's highly disciplined days, is no mere stopgap. With fine section leaders, rather than stars, as soloists, this is a genuinely integrated performance. And Szell's section leaders, Rafael Druian and Abraham Skernik, were in any case stars in their own orchestral firmament. The coupling, a Sinfonia Concertante in the same key for four wind instruments and orchestra, may or may not have been composed by Mozart; but it is a good piece, well played by soloists from Eugene Ormandy's Philadelphia Orchestra (Sony SBK67177).

By the time he reached Idomeneo *at the age of 25, young Mozart had already composed ten operas, including* Mitridate, *a long, grandly serious, teenage prentice piece for Milan, and* La finta giardiniera, *a comedy containing foretastes of* Figaro's Wedding, *for Munich. These, however, are peripheral works, like the unfinished* Zaide *in which Mozart explored, but unfortunately discarded, the idea of setting spoken texts directly against orchestral accompaniment, as Beethoven would do later at a crucial point in* Fidelio. *For all their immaturity, they are nevertheless worth tracking down at adventurous music festivals, or in student productions, or, if it ever returns, in the musical firework display of* Mitridate *in a production sponsored by the Friends of Covent Garden for the Mozart bicentenary in 1991.*

Towering over all of these, however, stands Idomeneo, *the first opera to reveal Mozart's powers at full throttle, his grasp of operatic structure startlingly assured, his psychological insight fast deepening, his vision of the eighteenth-century Enlightenment throwing its beams far beyond his native Salzburg. Although, in our own day, it has taken long to establish itself alongside* Figaro *and the later masterpieces, it has done so at last. The Mozart authority, Edward J. Dent, once called it a work always to be attended 'in a spirit of pilgrimage'. In 1934, this pilgrimage was to Glasgow, where its British premiere was given by Glasgow's amateur Grand Opera Society conducted by Erik Chisholm. Like Berlioz's by no means dissimilar* The Trojans, *of which Chisholm conducted the British premiere the following year, it remains a very special piece, a performance of which is always an event.*

Three

1781
IDOMENEO, RE DI CRETA, K366

Opera seria in three acts, to a libretto by Giambattista Varesco

The difference between *opera seria* and *opera buffa*, it is said, is that in *opera seria* ('serious opera') the characters are either mythological or historical, whereas in *opera buffa* ('comic opera') they are real people, especially if the composer is Mozart. Or, to put it another way, in *opera seria* the singers stand still and declaim, whereas in *opera buffa* they move around and converse. So, when Glyndebourne staged its first momentous and revelatory *Idomeneo* at the Edinburgh Festival in 1953, and every member of the cast kept moving, the production was widely criticised as being false to eighteenth-century style. Today, when movement is the least of the falsehoods applied to *opera seria* by progressive stage directors, it can be said that opera has entered an entirely different phase in its history.

In 1953, *opera seria* was still regarded as the difficult, more didactic and moribund side of Mozart's operatic output, which was why it had to be presented 'accessibly' (a word not actually applied to the arts in Britain until many years later, by which time accessibility, like anti-elitism, had become a public credo). Yet Mozart, as did Rossini and Donizetti after him, composed many more 'serious' operas more often than comedies; it was just that the comedies appealed more directly to modern taste, were easier to sing, and therefore were more frequently performed.

For years, *La clemenza di Tito*, written alongside *The Magic Flute* just before Mozart's death, was deemed a dodo, the work of a composer whose inspiration was flagging. Yet *The Magic Flute*, far from being a product of flagging inspiration, was a deserved and instant hit, both comic and sublime. It was simply that *Tito*, at least during the first half of the twentieth century, was misunderstood. Today, however, attitudes to Mozart's serious operas have changed. *Tito* has regained acceptance, and *Idomeneo* has come to seem the acme of *opera seria*, not a stilted, tedious essay in an outmoded style but a living, persuasive, moving music drama, inspired enough to be hailed by one admirably reckless authority as Mozart's greatest opera.

When the invitation to write it came from Munich in 1780, it provided Mozart with an irresistible opportunity to compose a work truly worthy of himself and at the same time, or so he hoped, to rid himself permanently of his increasingly irksome Salzburg duties. The first objective he achieved at speed; the second followed soon afterwards, though not quite in the way he had anticipated. Since writing *Idomeneo* meant residing in Munich for some months, his hope was that the move might become permanent.

Munich was an increasingly intellectual, sophisticated city, to which Mannheim's model opera and drama company, complete with the greatest orchestra in Europe, had recently moved.

Mozart could well have prospered there, but the job he desired never materialised. Instead, it was to fickle Vienna that the by then vulnerable freelance composer gravitated. Not that *Idomeneo* proved simplicity to compose, in spite of the quality of the opera company at his disposal. The cast he was offered was more variable than what he would find in Vienna, with a protagonist too old for the role. His librettist was a Salzburg-based routinier – a cleric in the cathedral – whose text required constant attention.

But the work itself triumphed over adversity. Mozart seized every opportunity to make it the greatest *opera seria* ever written – not stiffly formal but thoroughly flexible, emotionally forceful, structurally continuous, unprecedentedly atmospheric in its wealth of orchestral detail and colour of a sort which Gluck, for all his operatic reforms, could not have matched, and which Mozart himself, for that matter, never surpassed. The way he could bring about a radical change of mood simply through the tiniest of changes in instrumental timbre was one of his most conspicuous achievements in this opera.

The story, a variation on the heartfelt plight of Jephtha, likewise suited Mozart to perfection. The titular hero, far from being some cold cardboard king, is quickly given flesh and blood when he finds himself facing the cruellest of fates. Returning to Crete from the Trojan War, his ship almost founders in a storm. Only a prayer to Neptune can save him, but the malevolent sea-god's terms are ruthless. Idomeneo must sacrifice the first person he encounters on reaching land. That person turns out to be Idamante, his own son, whom he has not seen for twenty years.

Mozart handles Idomeneo's predicament, and his attempt to evade the inevitable, with fierce drama and pathos. The sea-monster which the impatient Neptune dispatches to the island to speed him into action brings the opera's central act to a climax in reverse – the tense *prestissimo* music grows quieter and quieter as the people flee in terror. The entire work is filled with such masterstrokes of subtlety, which the audience at the Munich court must have been sophisticated enough to savour.

The two women who love young Idamante, and who thus complicate the issue of his fate, are as psychologically opposed in character as they are identical in resolve. How Mozart develops and criss-crosses their personalities is another example of the new command of operatic form, and of expressive recitative, he had gained since writing the exquisite but undramatic music of *Il re pastore* in Salzburg five years earlier. Even the ending, which follows the conventions of *opera seria* by being happy, is in keeping with the nature of the drama that leads to it. Idamante stays alive, but Idomeneo loses his throne. The virtues of reason and tolerance emerge victorious. The old order gives way to the new. By the standards of *opera seria*, but even more so those of the Enlightenment, it is no mere compromise but an anticipation of *The Magic Flute*.

When Glyndebourne staged *Idomeneo* in 1953, it employed a tenor Idamante, necessitating the downward transposition of a role originally written for castrato voice (another *opera seria* convention) and dulling the bright edge of Mozart's music. Today, the use of a soprano or mezzo-soprano in what works perfectly well as a Mozartian 'breeches role' is the preferred solution to the problem. Most recordings do it this way; and, with Anne Sofie von Otter in the part, Sir John Eliot Gardiner's 1990 recording starts with a considerable advantage. Moreover, with Anthony Rolfe Johnson as the most human of kings, and Sylvia McNair and Hillevi Martinpelto as the rival women, this is a tellingly cast performance, rivetingly supported by Gardiner's own Monteverdi Choir and the period instruments of the English Baroque Soloists (DG Archiv 431 674-2).

Not even Sir Charles Mackerras quite rivals it in his more recent recording, which forms part of his fine Mozart cycle made in Edinburgh with the Scottish Chamber Orchestra. In the title role, Ian Bostridge cannot quite conceal his youthfulness; and the recording, made in the Usher Hall, brings a disturbing edginess to some of the voices. Of Mackerras's conducting, however, there can be no such criticism. The dramatic colours of the music, as well as its moments of serenity, are at his fingertips, along with his deep appreciation of Mozartian style (EMI 7243 5 57260 2).

Four

1784
SERENADE IN B FLAT MAJOR FOR THIRTEEN WIND INSTRUMENTS, K361

Largo – Allegro molto   Menuetto – Trio 1 and 2   Adagio

Menuetto (Allegretto) – Trio 1 and 2

Romanze (Adagio – Allegretto – Adagio)

Thema mit variationem (Andante)   Finale (Molto allegro)

Mozart's B flat major Wind Serenade, K361, is the big one. Also known as the *Gran Partita*, or 'Grand Suite', it is scored for the most elaborate of wind ensembles, laid out in the greatest number of movements, and held in the highest awe by devotees of classical wind music. Yet, unlike his two other mature wind serenades, the E flat major, K375, and the C minor, K388, which were commissioned from Mozart by rich Viennese patrons, its origin long seemed obscure, its lavishness a mystery.

For many years, indeed, it was thought not to date from Mozart's Viennese years at all, but to be a masterpiece of earlier vintage. The source of its sumptuous instrumentation seemed to lie not in Austria at all but in the city of Munich, which in 1780 had commissioned Mozart to compose *Idomeneo*, his greatest *opera seria*, and had placed at his disposal the finest imaginable orchestra to perform it in January 1781. Among the orchestra's assets were four horns, rather than just the usual pair, and Mozart already knew what he could do with such a quartet, tuned in two different ways. He had used this facility to high effect in his Symphony No. 25 in G minor, K183, the best of all his early symphonies; and he made fresh use of it not only in *Idomeneo* but also in this stupendous wind serenade, K361.

Yet the serenade's Munich connection remained purely speculative. The vital evidence was missing. Nobody yet knew why, or where, Mozart actually wrote it. The most plausible suggestion was that he may have begun it in Munich in the spring of 1781 and finished it later in Vienna, after his final break with the oppressive Archbishop of Salzburg. There was no doubt that Munich meant much to him, and that the months he spent there supervising *Idomeneo* were happy and busy ones. It was not too far from provincial Salzburg, yet far enough for him to be out of reach of his father and of the Salzburg court, which was increasingly frustrating him. If he had won a permanent appointment there, his subsequent career might have been very different.

But 1781 in any case marked a watershed in his life when, as he personally reported, he left Salzburg 'with a kick on my arse by order of our worthy Prince Archbishop'. He was still in his mid-twenties; his career as an independent, and infinitely more ambitious, composer in Vienna was beginning; and the Serenade, K361, now seems to look more and more like one of its manifestations. Its style was more splendid, more inventive and resourceful than that of his little Salzburg wind divertimentos, and its colouring was greatly richer. Yet, wherever he wrote it, the sound of the Munich orchestra, with its four horns and peerless woodwind, was surely in his ears.

There was also, however, another sound, a very novel one, which was that of the basset horn, an instrument peculiar to Vienna and to one particular player, Mozart's new friend Anton Stadler. Since Mozart had never written for basset horns before, and since their role in this serenade (where he employed a pair of them) is so important, the work's Viennese identity seems more or less established.

But there was one further fact which is now considered to clinch the matter and to fix the date of composition. On 23 March 1784, a Viennese newspaper announced that 'Today Herr Stadler senior, at present in the service of His Majesty the Emperor, will give a musical academy [i.e. concert] for his benefit in the Imperial Royal National Court Theatre, at which, among other well-chosen pieces, a large wind work of a very special kind by Herr Mozart will be performed'.

The work could only have been this one, even if a commentator at the time threw researchers off the scent by reporting that it contained just four movements (but then perhaps it was not performed complete). The commentator's identification of the instruments taking part, and his description of what he heard – 'glorious and grand, excellent and sublime' – proclaims surely that he had been listening to a performance of the Serenade for Thirteen Wind Instruments in which, as still happens today, the double bassoon was replaced by a string bass.

The B flat is, unquestionably, Mozart's most sublime serenade, though not necessarily his greatest; that accolade surely goes to K388 in C minor, a work of incomparable black intensity of expression, though hardly a serenade within the normal meaning of the word. Much of K361, on the other hand, is exquisitely nocturnal, though it is also imposingly symphonic and emotionally complex – a long and copious score, built on the same huge scale as the 'Haffner' serenade for full orchestra, though much more profound in its inspiration.

The first movement, complete with an expressive slow introduction out of whose succulent opening chords the sound of a solo clarinet tenderly untwines, immediately suggests its spaciousness of design. The first of the two minuets, too, is elaborately worked, with two contrasted trio sections, the first of them in E flat major for a cluster of clarinets and basset horns, the second in Mozart's emotive key of G minor, darker and more mysterious.

By this point, the music's emphasis on contrast – between euphony and energy, sweetness and pungency, reedy oboes and creamy clarinets – has fully established itself. The third movement, a pulsating and haunting *adagio*, is the work's most complete stroke of genius — a slow, amorous song for oboe, clarinet and basset horn, almost operatic in its eloquence, voiced above a syncopated, hesitantly murmuring accompaniment.

The second minuet, again with two contrasted trio sections, breaks the spell. It is robustly genial, but is followed by a second *adagio*, emotionally ambiguous, opening meditatively but soon interrupted by a tense, troubled, faster middle section in the minor. The high point of the sixth movement, a theme with six variations, comes towards the end in a lovely slow oboe solo, accompanied by swaying basset horns.

A circling, insistently raucous rondo, full of cackling glee, then ties the whole work together. With its unmistakable 'Turkishness', a fashionable musical exoticism popular in Vienna at the time, this finale is suggestive of *Die Entführung aus dem Serail* ('The Abduction from the Seraglio'), Mozart's first Viennese opera, with its strongly Turkish plot. The opera's date, 1782, and the fact that Anton Stadler was a member of the orchestra, provides further evidence that the B flat Serenade belongs to Mozart's Vienna years.

Though the lowest of the thirteen instruments specified by Mozart was in fact a string bass rather than a double bassoon, this is generally thought to be because the eighteenth-century double bassoon was so unreliable. Players today decide for themselves which instrument to choose, and some performances — most famously those which Otto Klemperer conducted — employ both. The work's alternative title, *Gran Partita*, is unauthentic.

The inscription, in red ink, on the autograph score is not in Mozart's handwriting. But the name is perfectly apt.

Since all who love the B flat Serenade know just how they like it to sound, finding the right recording can be difficult. Neville Marriner's bargain-price issue, with members of the Academy of St Martin in the Fields, is much savoured for its bold colours and warmth of tone. The inclusion of the glorious E flat major Wind Serenade, K375, played by the Heinz Holliger Ensemble, is no mere filler but a masterpiece in its own right (Philips 446 227-2PM).

Five

1782
SERENADE IN C MINOR FOR WIND OCTET, K388

Allegro   Andante   Menuetto   Allegro

'Let me tell you', wrote the 25-year-old Mozart to his father soon after settling in Vienna in 1781, 'that at table the other day the emperor gave me the very highest praise.' Though the letter did not put the anxious Leopold's fears at rest about the well-being of his son, Mozart was already producing enough fine music – including this exceptional C minor Serenade for two oboes, two clarinets, two bassoons and two horns – to make his dramatic move from the security of Salzburg to the risks of the Austrian capital seem worthwhile. Aristocratic listeners were impressed with him, or so he hoped, and commissions were flowing in. The one for the C minor Serenade came in 1782 from a certain Prince Liechtenstein, who was forming a wind band and wanted a piece of *Tafelmusik* ('entertainment music') in a hurry. 'Not much to be expected from that quarter', Mozart astutely remarked at the time. He was allowed two days in which to write the piece.

Given the light-heartedness of its title – Mozart also described it as a 'Nacht Musique' – the work might have been expected to be as charmingly inconsequential as anyone else's eighteenth-century serenade. The choice of a potentially sombre minor key, on the other hand, suggests otherwise. Even Mozart's slightest works have a habit of overriding their original intentions, or the terms of their commission – and there is no doubt that this is very different from most of his other serenades. When his father, recalling the performance of one such work in the open air on a summer evening outside the house of a Salzburg friend, remarked that 'we knew nothing about it until we heard it deliciously in our rooms from across the water', we can be sure it was not K388 he was referring to.

There is no frippery about this music, nothing 'delicious' about this edgy, acidic work. Unlike traditional classical serenades, it does not open with a jolly march. Its first notes are abrasively stark, a summary rather than a summery call to attention. The oboe tone rasps. The mellowness of Mozart's favourite clarinets seems subdued. The impatient rhythms contain an ominous foretaste of the first movement of Beethoven's Fifth Symphony, written twenty-six years later in the same key. If, as has been suggested, Mozart had manic-depressive tendencies, a sombre serenade might be thought to confirm the fact.

Though the slow movement in E flat major brings some moments of balm, stridency resumes in the minuet, which – no ordinary dance movement – is a contrapuntal hotbed of discords. Technical descriptions of its devices – canon at the double octave for oboes and bassoons, double canon at the fourth by inversion, with the second oboe being answered by the first and the first bassoon by the second – give no impression of the searing intensity of this music, in which the character of a courtly minuet is attacked from all sides. The French Revolution, it should be remembered, was just a few years away, and that most subversive of comic operas, *Figaro's Wedding*, was also in the offing.

More than one Mozart authority has asked how it was possible that such an outburst of negative feeling could have pleased a prince and his dinner guests in the way they expected. Perhaps they never even noticed, though it must be said that Prince Liechtenstein thereafter never commissioned another work from Mozart. All that the composer himself reported, in a letter to his father, was that he had had to write the work for wind instruments, because the prince had no strings in his entourage.

But such is the mystery of genius – and the finale provides little enlightenment. A set of variations, it opens with all the minor-key abrasiveness of the first movement; but a swing to E flat major, glowingly signalled by the horns, begins to slacken the tension, paving the way for a C major ending that may – or more probably may not – be meant to prove that Mozart, earlier in the work, was merely teasing.

Some of the best recordings of this serenade are locked into complete, or at least substantial, collections of Mozart's wind music, occupying anything up to six discs. Listeners fearing such an acquisition to be a bit specialised – though there are good reasons for taking the plunge – should therefore seek a recording in which the C minor Serenade is coupled on a single disc with its emotional obverse, the lighter, slightly earlier E flat major Serenade, K375, for the same octet of wind instruments. Indeed, there is no better way to come to terms with the terse, dark grandeur of the C minor masterpiece than to hear it in the context of the warm, more leisurely E flat major. The English Concert Winds provide this opportunity on an excellent disc which also includes wind versions of the overtures to *Figaro's Wedding*, *Don Giovanni* and *The Magic Flute* (Hyperion CDA 66887).

Had Haydn and Mozart been father and son, which in terms of their dates and places of birth would have been not impossible, would Mozart's musical career have developed very differently from how it did? For a start, it would be safe to say that he would not have been toured round Europe as a wunderkind. His musical education would have been more private, less internationally sophisticated, though no less thorough. Perhaps — who knows? — he would have lived as long as Haydn himself, and worked in Vienna alongside Beethoven and Schubert, whose music his own so often anticipated.

What we do know is that Haydn and Mozart hugely admired each other, the older composer learning as much from the younger as the younger from the older. With Mozart as his son, Haydn might have composed better operas and better concertos. What Mozart certainly learned from Haydn was how to write string quartets. Haydn, in his set of six quartets, Op. 33, and their predecessors, the so-called Sun quartets, Op. 20, had developed and perfected the art by the time he was in his late forties and Mozart in his mid-twenties. And it was Mozart's experience of Haydn's Op. 33 which made him decide to compose a similar set of his own, dedicating it to the older master in recognition of his genius. Before that time, Mozart had produced good but uninspired string quartets. In his six Haydn quartets, as they came to be known, he produced great ones.

They were works in which he perfected his own approach to the form and over which he took special pains, as their manuscripts clearly show. The traditional belief that Mozart composed effortlessly is swept aside by the sight of them. Corrections are everywhere. Tempo and dynamic markings are crossed out and altered. The engraver's plates contain further alterations. So much for what has long been hailed as Mozart's sublime spontaneity. But what he put into these quartets is what, very definitely, we now get out of them.

Six

1783
STRING QUARTET IN D MINOR, K421

Allegro   Andante

Menuetto: Allegretto   Allegretto ma non troppo

Of the set of six quartets which Mozart famously completed and dedicated to Haydn in 1785, the D minor is the darkest. Its poignancy, its passion, its sudden switches between loud and soft tone, its startling chromaticisms all point the way to the quartet in the same key that Schubert was to write forty years later. Had Mozart chosen to call his work 'Death and the Maiden', the spectral equestrian rhythms of the finale would doubtless have inspired essays on the supernatural aspects of his music. D minor, after all, was the key of *Don Giovanni*, as well as of the unfinished Requiem and, in its first movement at least, the most demonic of his piano concertos.

Certainly, the D minor Quartet is a work that only briefly brightens – in the central trio section of the minuet – and even there the brightness could be compared with the brightness of tears. Unlike the C major Quartet, K465, which ends in comedy after a disconcertingly chromatic and forward-looking introduction, its intentions from first note to last are constantly to disturb. Mozart himself was disturbed while writing it. Constanze, his wife, was in labour at the time, and she claimed later that her cries had been composed into the music. The loud, harsh octave leaps that suddenly intrude upon the quietness of the slow movement are usually thought to be the passage she referred to. To suggest – as nineteenth-century commentators sometimes did – that the music also foretold the child's death two months later may seem to be over-fanciful. Yet D minor, on all the evidence, was Mozart's key of destiny, and one to which he turned only when the occasion strongly demanded it.

The six *Haydn* quartets were undoubtedly works over which he took special pains. But then, these were works about which he was peculiarly self-conscious. For a start, he intended to dedicate them to Haydn, Vienna's senior genius, and he wrote them only after a deep study of Haydn's own set of six quartets, Op. 33. Mozart wanted – indeed needed – Haydn's admiration, and he received it in a nicely worded tribute, delivered to the former wunderkind's father at an evening of chamber music when three of the new quartets were performed.

Haydn's response has gone down in history. 'Before God and as an honest man,' he declared, 'I tell you that your son is the greatest composer known to me either in person or by name. He has taste and, what is more, the most profound knowledge of composition.' On a subsequent occasion, the two composers met to play quartets together, Haydn on first violin, Mozart on viola, with two other composers, Dittersdorf and Vanhal, forming the rest of the ensemble. The singer, Michael Kelly, who was present, remarked that they played well enough 'but by no means extraordinarily'. So much for the opinions of singers. Michael Kelly did not know his luck.

The mood of the D minor Quartet is sombrely explicit. Leaps or descents of an octave or more characterise all four movements and contribute to their air of restlessness. The first of these, *sotto voce*, forms the work's opening notes and is the most persistent feature of the first movement's grimly grinding main theme. The shading of the music throughout owes much of its subtlety to the way in which the second violin and viola parts are written. The variations of the andante similarly gain their touches of genius from the most deceptively simple of means, in this case the use of little rests, which keep halting the progress of an otherwise flowing movement.

Mozart's minuets in minor keys have been described as possessing a sort of 'courageous sadness' – words appropriate to this D minor example, and not at all contradicted by the D major sweetness of the trio section. The finale possesses this quality, too, especially in the little repeated notes, high on the first violin, that form the tail of the main theme and ultimately, after a tempo increase, bring the movement to its close. Again the material is of the utmost simplicity, but the effect is deeply touching, as only Mozart can be.

If Mozart's *Haydn* quartets are musical dialogues of the most sublime sort – they are also much else – then the recordings by the French-based Quatuor Mosaïques catch this aspect of them to perfection. Every voice makes its point as part of a beautifully balanced entity. In their intimacy of expression, these performances show that period instruments in the right hands lack nothing in rich intensity or keen responsiveness to the music's riveting repartee. These are revelatory performances in every sense of the word, all the better for never sounding overpressed in the modern manner.

Since the discs are available separately at bargain price, the works can be bought in pairs. The D minor Quartet is coupled with the one that forms Mozart's introduction to the set, the witty and effervescent G major, K387, with its suddenly deeply serious slow movement (Astree Naïve E8843). But, once you have bought this, you will want the others, too, in order to get a complete picture of these varied masterpieces and to escape from the deplorable concert-hall practice whereby Mozart's and Haydn's quartets are almost invariably treated as curtain-raisers.

As a fascinating alternative to the Quatuor Mosaïques, the three-disc boxed set, also at bargain price, by Germany's remarkable Hagen Quartet approaches the six works from an entirely different angle (DG 471 024-2). These are players accustomed to performing the post-Mozart repertoire up to Bartók and beyond, and they play Mozart, as it were, with hindsight, showing how he anticipated Beethoven, Schubert – and, for that matter, Bartók (listen to how they feel their way into the soft opening discords of the *Dissonance* quartet). The record-collector who can afford both these sets will end up with a comprehensive knowledge of Mozart's *Haydn* quartets – and who can say better than that?

Seven

1785
PIANO CONCERTO IN C MAJOR, K467

Allegro maestoso   Andante   Allegro vivace assai

When a Mozart piano concerto finds its way into the soundtrack of a romantic film, its effect can be to take you completely by surprise and, as a result, hit you hard. This is what happened towards the end of *The French Lieutenant's Woman*. But the magic worked still more potently in Bo Widerberg's sentimental Swedish tragedy, *Elvira Madigan*, through the stealthy presence of the slow movement of the C major Piano Concerto, K467. It was the music's atmosphere, of course, which did the trick. To a degree unmatched in any of Mozart's other works, a haunting iridescence steals through this andante – and thus also through the film – in a peculiarly palpitating form, whereby the softest, most fine-spun of themes receives the most muted yet restless of accompaniments.

The nocturnal hush of the string tone, the ascents and descents of the melody, the sudden little stabs of pain, the delayed entry of the piano, the aching modulations, the operatic leaps of the very vocal melodic line from one register to another, the chromatic poignancy, the disturbing dissonances and the sweetness with which they are resolved, are all contributory factors to the strange, dreamlike beauty and trembling rapture of the music – and to what can only be called the mystery that is Mozart.

Every tiny detail makes its point in a way that the notes on the printed page scarcely hint at. Every delicate stroke, every phrase length, every change of colour is similarly dumbfounding. The expected Mozartian interplay between piano and orchestra is almost entirely missing. The piano, once it has made its entry, is there for keeps – or almost for keeps, because there is a brief moment when it is disquietingly absent. It is music which, on its own abstract terms, seems to possess some sort of veiled subject matter, which Widerberg was acute enough to perceive and make use of.

Yet this movement, extraordinary though it is, is in no way out of keeping with the rest of the work, or with other Mozart concertos of the period – a particularly fertile one in concerto terms, thanks to the series of sub-scription concerts upon which he had embarked in 1784. Most of these masterpieces had brilliant and subtle solo parts intended for himself to play. The sheer splendour of the opening movement, however, surpasses any of its predecessors in the way a characteristically simple marchlike rhythm is employed as a basis for majestic and spacious development.

Not until Mozart entered this concerto in his personal catalogue of his works (a list he had only recently begun to compile) did he decide to add the word 'maestoso' to the tempo-marking. It is a description with which some pianists have felt uneasy, in spite of the presence of ceremonial trumpets and drums in the scoring, because they believe the music should move more quickly than the term 'maestoso' implies.

But the interplay between soloist and orchestra, for all its wit, possesses a grander-than-usual symphonic dimension which was to become still grander in the first movement of a later C major concerto (K503) and which surely justifies Mozart's use of the term. Yet lightness of touch is present also, and should never be sacrificed for the sake of a majesty which, according to some soloists, does not here exist. It is in the balance between the two sides of this movement that the secret of the music surely lies.

No such problems exist in the finale, which, after the troubled tranquillity of the andante, moves instantly into action like some sort of galvanised gavotte. In fact, the music – like most concerto finales of the period – is a rondo, but one whose energy and impetus anticipate that of Beethoven's C major Piano Concerto of ten years later. The links between Mozart's C major concertos K467 and 503 and Beethoven's concerto in the same key are indeed quite striking, though nobody should make the mistake of listening to (or, worse, playing) the one composer in terms of the other. The shadows which occasionally cross the flashing surface of Mozart's finale are entirely his own.

In the perceptive words of the concert pianist Charles Rosen, K467 is a work which, along with its D minor predecessor, K466, represents 'a liberation of the genre, a demonstration that the concerto could stand with equal dignity beside any other musical form, capable of expressing the same depth of feeling and of working out the most complex musical idea'. This is not something that could be said with such conviction about Haydn's concertos, peerless symphonist though he was; but it fits Mozart's like a glove.

But if Widerberg's film has helped people to discover K467, it has come at a price. To nickname the concerto *Elvira Madigan*, as now happens all the time, is merely to vulgarise it. Add to this the gross over-exposure of the slow movement on radio and television, and the music itself begins to sound tainted. The fault is not Mozart's but simply the inescapable ubiquity of background music, which has reduced even Mahler's Eighth Symphony – which used to be a once-in-a-lifetime experience – to the routine of a regular event.

Yet a fine performance of K467 can alter everything and revive the most jaded of musical palates. Among recordings, Maria João Pires's is one of those that can do so, the first movement being neither too pompous nor too flippant, the slow movement projecting moonlit radiance without a drop of saccharine, the finale keen and witty.

Murray Perahia's, Alfred Brendel's and Geza Anda's are other recordings worth mentioning. But Pires scores by coupling K467 with the silvery G major Piano Concerto, K453, usually described as a woman's work – Mozart wrote it for his pupil Barbara Ployer – but sounding all the better for being articulated by Pires's firm yet sensitive fingers. Recorded live in

Italy, the music features Claudio Abbado and the Chamber Orchestra of Europe in vivacious form, and without too much distracting audience noise (DG 439 941-2).

For total freshness of sonority, however, no performance surpasses Malcolm Bilson's on a lightweight Mozartian fortepiano, with John Eliot Gardiner and the English Baroque Soloists supplying taut, lucid support. The coupling this time is the concerto's immediate and very different predecessor, the passionate D minor, K466, which loses nothing, and gains much, from a performance which demonstrates musical authenticity at its best (DG 419 609-2).

Eight

1785
QUARTET FOR PIANO AND STRINGS IN
G MINOR, K478

Allegro   Andante   Rondo: Allegro moderato

In 1785, the year he began composing *Figaro's Wedding*, Mozart was commissioned by the publisher Hoffmeister to write three quartets for piano
and strings. It was a novel idea. There was no important precedent for
such music. There were no earlier works of their kind in Mozart's output.
He had, or so it seemed, *carte blanche* to do what he liked. And the first of
the quartets, in G minor, showed him rising to the challenge with what
was not quite a piano concerto but not at all the cosy piece of musical
domesticity which the publisher, as it turned out, must have expected
from him. Hoffmeister promptly withdrew from the contract, declaring
the work 'too difficult'. So Mozart placed his next quartet, the E flat major,
which was even more of a piano concerto, in the more sympathetic hands
of Artaria and Company, but by then he was clearly losing interest in the

project. Thanks to Hoffmeister's lack of enthusiasm, the third quartet was never composed.

Of course the music was difficult, both to play and interpret. That was what it was meant to be. Mozart's more public works of the period – the D minor Piano Concerto, K466, or the E flat major, K482 – were in safe hands, especially if they were his own. But in the case of his more domestic music, his general willingness to accept the deficiencies of amateur pianists – especially if they happened to be attractive young women – was diminishing as he moved more and more into the writing of works which were introspective rather than entertaining.

In this respect, the two piano quartets were among the turning points in his output. What would one of his pupils have made of the G minor masterpiece, K478? At that moment in his life, when he had reached the grand, mature age of 29, he probably did not much care. The music had been written, and those who got access to it could make of it what they liked. Mozart in 1785 was no trivialist and, though he was aware his publishers liked works which were user-friendly – or, as they put it, which 'could hold their own when performed with average skill' – he was increasingly unwilling to write to order for a Viennese public who would in any case have preferred the sweet nothings of a composer such as Pleyel.

But there was another aspect of these two works which set them apart from others of their kind. They actually merged Mozart's private world with his public one in the sense that they seemed to belong to his chamber output and his orchestral output at one and the same time. The concerto-like characteristics of the piano parts were difficult enough to daunt would-be players, but the intimacy of the string writing – for violin, viola and cello – had a quality quite different from that of the piano concertos.

It was a potent and wholly individual mixture, but it took people a long time to recognise the fact. And before they did so, Mozart had stopped writing piano quartets. The ones he did write were the *crème de la crème* – 'the only absolutely perfect, great, deep masterpieces of their problematic genre', as that ever-perceptive Mozart authority, Hans Keller of the BBC, once put it – and are never more recognisably so than when presented together in a single concert.

Heard thus, the contrasts between the warmth of Mozart's response to the key of E flat major and the sombreness he brought to G minor – that most disturbing of all his keys – make their full effect. Yet the differences between them are not as simple as that. The brilliant, clear-cut colours of the first movement of the E flat major masterpiece have a way of clouding over, the music showing increasing leanings towards the minor, in the way it does in the great major-key piano concertos of the same period. The darkness of the viola tone keeps adding shadows to the brightness of the violin, penetrating the calm of the lingering larghetto with a recurring sense of introspection, without in the end destroying the music's Viennese glow.

But, in the G minor, the glow is more heavily under threat. The passionate gloom of the opening bars speaks for itself. What domestic ensemble in Mozart's time would have wanted to perform it, what audience to listen to it? A death-consciousness – indeed a death knell – sounds ominously through those stark, hollow opening notes in octaves, in a way that would have repelled most amateur performers of the period. Even when the music moves into the major, the threat is still there.

Nor does it recede in the lyricism – what some would call the love music – of the B flat major slow movement, even if it takes a different form in phrases so meltingly moulded that it aches with knowledge of life's – or love's – transitoriness. Again it is the sound world of the great piano concertos, and of the operas, which is encountered here, reduced to its essence in passages where the piano tone interweaves with first one string instrument, then with another.

If the music switches from G minor to G major in the finale, as if to prove that its troubles are over, this was a tactic that Mozart had employed more than once before, not least in the D minor Piano Concerto, though never with the simplistic effect of supplying what merely seemed a self-consciously happy ending. The major-key finale of the G minor Piano Quartet is just one more masterstroke, its operatic beauty never less than touching, and throwing the rest of the work into high relief.

Though these works in our own time have had plenty of champions, the most welcome recordings are those which have coupled them on a single disc. The one by Isaac Stern, Jaime Laredo and Yo Yo Ma, with Emanuel Ax as pianist (Sony SMK 89794) is as classy as anyone could hope for – Mozart himself would surely have been amazed by it. Yet its starriness does not result in superficiality or ostentation.

These are performances that probe every nuance of the music. However, they are undeniably big-boned, especially in terms of piano tone, and listeners desiring a less aggressive approach are recommended to the lovely Clifford Curzon recording with members of the Amadeus Quartet, none the worse for being half a century old (Decca 425 960-2). Both discs are budget price, but the latter has the advantage of including, as an extra, the Horn Quintet in E flat major, K407, with the incomparable Dennis Brain as hornist.

For something utterly fresh, however, Paul Lewis's recording of the two quartets with the Leopold String Trio, issued as these pages go to press, is all that could be desired. An offshoot of a millennial Edinburgh Festival concert, this is Mozart playing of the highest calibre and clarity of focus, showing why, in 2003, Lewis – a pupil of Alfred Brendel – was instrumentalist of the year in the Royal Philharmonic Society awards (Hyperion CDA 67373).

Nine

1786
PIANO CONCERTO IN C MINOR, K491

Allegro   Larghetto   Allegretto

Most of Mozart's piano concertos have been described for various reasons as 'unique'; but some, it could be said, are more unique than others. Allowing for the misuse of the word – Mozart, after all, composed almost thirty such works – what is it that makes the C minor Concerto so special? First, it is the only one he composed in that key, and is one of only two he composed in the minor. Moreover, it is the only Mozart concerto that ends as well as begins in the minor (the D minor Concerto, K466, closes merrily in the major).

But there is something else – less frequently acknowledged by commentators – which makes it different. This is the fact that the stark and stealthy opening theme employs all twelve notes of the chromatic scale. So melodious is this pre-Schoenbergian feature of the music that it passes unnoticed, in the same way as does the melodic twelve-note row on which Britten's opera, *The Turn of the Screw*, is based. The difference is that Mozart did it in 1786, before twelve-note rows were common currency, and it so fascinated the twentieth-century German composer Giselher Klebe that he used Mozart's theme as a twelve-note series in an atonal symphony for strings written in 1953.

The writing of the C minor Piano Concerto so preoccupied Mozart during one of the busiest periods in his career that he interrupted the composition of *Figaro's Wedding* to make way for it in the spring of 1786. One of the greatest of his magnificent series of Viennese concertos, it was first played by Mozart himself at a concert in the Burgtheater, a month before the premiere of the opera in the same surroundings. The performance marked what was to be his last major appearance as a solo pianist. The fickle Viennese had heard enough of his virtuosity; and, though three more concertos still lay ahead, he was by then 'losing ground', as a recent biographer has put it, and was 'no longer needed' as a concert performer.

Yet Beethoven, on first hearing the C minor Concerto, famously said: 'Ah, we shall never be able to do anything like this' – though he could not refrain from writing a concerto of his own in C minor, a key which came to mean as much to him as it had done to Mozart. When performed in a portentous nineteenth-century manner, Mozart's concerto can itself be made to sound quite Beethovenian, even if to do so is invariably to distort it. Beethoven's playing of it would have been fascinating to hear.

Whether we should think of it as a 'tragic' concerto, on the other hand, rather depends on what can be said to constitute tragedy in a piece of abstract classical music. But the trustworthy Alfred Brendel, a devotee of this work, has had no more difficulty than the less-than-trustworthy Alfred Einstein in recognising this concerto as tragic in quality. Indeed, he has called it 'the tragic piece par excellence', adding that it is the most contrapuntally dense of all Mozart's concertos. And though it would be a mistake to claim that minor keys and density of counterpoint automatically signify tragedy – more often than not they don't – in the case of this concerto it somehow all adds up. Mozart employed minor keys so rarely that they invariably draw attention to themselves. It all depends, however, on what you hear as tragedy, and on whether you sense a connection between this work and the C minor Fantasia, K475, for solo piano – a shorter, less ambitious tragedy, but not to be underrated.

Certainly there is a ghostly pathos about the first movement, with its painfully stabbing dissonances, just as there is something strangely wraithlike about the progress of the finale through its series of six mostly restrained but gripping variations. Proceeding like a stealthy yet inexorable march, to which the mirthlessly dancing measures of the closing pages add no shred of comfort, this set of variations seems all the more disturbing after the softly sunlit relief of the slow movement in E flat major, with its lovely woodwind detail.

Yet the innocent main theme of this gentle larghetto, absurdly simple though it sounds, is made as treacherous as a sheet of ice through the small rhythmic changes incorporated in each of its repetitions. Should it be played exactly as written? Or should the pianist decorate it, and, if so, to what extent?

Again, Alfred Brendel seems to hold the key to Mozart's mind. His recording with Sir Charles Mackerras and the Scottish Chamber Orchestra is exemplary in this as in all other respects, including fleetness of tempo, variety of colour, purity of articulation, and total rapport with a conductor whose handling of the music is sharp and vivid. In the absence of cadenzas by Mozart himself, Brendel plays his own – another exemplary feature of the performance. Happily, there are no problems here with the acoustical ambience of Edinburgh's Usher Hall, which never gets in the way of the playing (Philips 462 622-2).

With the D minor Concerto, K466, as the logical choice of coupling, this recording is in fact so good that there seems little point in recommending any other. If, however, you already have a disc of the D minor – though Brendel's would be worth possessing anyway – then Mitsuko Uchida's coupling of the C minor Concerto with the enchanting A major, K488, might be worth considering. But her playing, for all its beauty, can sound mannered in comparison with Brendel's, and Jeffrey Tate is tamer than Mackerras as conductor (Philips 442 648-2).

Ten

1786
LE NOZZE DI FIGARO, K492

Opera buffa in four acts to a libretto by Lorenzo da Ponte

In *Le mariage de Figaro*, Beaumarchais theatrically sowed some of the seeds of the French Revolution. When Mozart, collaborating for the first time with Lorenzo da Ponte as librettist, adapted it as an opera two years later, the play was still banned in Vienna, and the Revolution, which shook the whole of Europe, was approaching fast. How did they get away with their subversive musical comedy, the first great opera ever to have been based on a contemporary and audaciously relevant dramatic success?

In their favour, no doubt, was the fact that music sometimes deluded the censors in a way that the spoken word did not (though Verdi, half a century later, would find the going harder in Italy). Da Ponte's text in any case diluted the more inflammatory political aspects of the story, leaving Mozart's musical reintensifying of them to pass unnoticed amid much that was funny, sexually alluring and melodically diverting. Operatically, moreover, Vienna was undergoing change, and Mozart was part of it. His last major opera had been the dazzling *Die Entführung aus dem Serail* ('The Abduction from the Seraglio'), a comedy written in German for Vienna's National (German-speaking) Theatre in 1782, soon after his arrival in the city.

But when the theatre's imperial founder, Joseph II, decided to close it down and revert to Italian opera, Mozart saw his opportunity. Writing to his father in Salzburg, he said he had examined 100 or more Italian texts without yet finding the right one. After a few false starts – one of which, *The Goose of Cairo*, got dangerously far advanced – he hit upon the Beaumarchais play, which Emanuel Schikaneder (future librettist of *The Magic Flute*) had been banned from staging with his theatrical troupe. Would Mozart fare any better? He knew that the play's French predecessor, *The Barber of Seville*, had already been a Viennese hit in Paisiello's Italian operatic version. With true Mozartian *sang-froid*, he started work on *Figaro* in the autumn of 1785, and the work had its premiere, appropriately on May Day, at the Burgtheater in the spring of 1786.

Tales of the opera's failure, and of the damage it did to the composer's Viennese career, form part of the compendious Mozart mythology. The work was a success from the start, as confirmed by Joseph II's decree that the audience must cease interrupting it with demands for encores. Whatever intrigues there may have been against its political overtones did not come from the emperor, who was no more against *Figaro* than he had been against *Die Entführung*. His famous quizzical comment about the latter – 'Too many notes, my dear Mozart' – has always been erroneously translated. What he really said, if he ever said it at all, was 'An *extraordinary* number of notes', which was not quite the same thing.

Even if Viennese audiences generally preferred their comic operas to be lighter and frothier than *Figaro*, there is no doubt that this work, following the success of *Die Entführung*, fully established Mozart's theatrical reputation. With *Don Giovanni*, *Così fan tutte*, *La clemenza di Tito* and *The Magic Flute* still to come, his fame was spreading across Europe. Today, more than two centuries later, we go on adding to our love and knowledge of his operas. Even *Tito*, long regarded as retrogressive, seems sufficiently forward-looking to suggest that Mozart, three months before his death, was far from finished with the art of *opera seria*, which he had employed more inventively than any other composer. In all these works, his sureness of touch, his incomparable ability to shape a phrase, make an inspired modulation and strike a chord eloquently enough to turn the heart over, were aspects of his operatic genius that never deserted him.

From the first bar of the overture to *Figaro*, they are there in abundance. Though the music quotes, or pre-quotes, no theme from the opera itself, the raciness of what Beaumarchais had called a 'folle journée' ('crazy day') is fizzingly caught by the orchestra. Like all Mozart's mature overtures, it was composed after the rest of the work. This was by then deliberate

Mozart policy, enabling him to produce utterly appropriate introductory music, in this case reflecting at top speed the pell-mell events of a day in Count Almaviva's Spanish household.

It is different from his other mature overtures in that it has no slow introduction. As he recognised, any sort of interference with its breathless zest would have been counter-productive. Yet originally, before coming to that decision, he did write down a slow minor-key interlude that would have extended the overture by sixty-four bars. A first graceful bar of this andante, marked to be played by oboe and pizzicato strings, is all that survives, suggesting perhaps an intention to evoke the Countess Almaviva's lonely awareness that her husband is wooing not only her own chambermaid, Susanna, but also the gardener's under-age daughter, Barbarina.

Since it is Susanna, rather than the Countess, who emerges as the opera's heroine, and it is Figaro, the Count's barber, rather than the Count himself, who is the hero, the original audience must have been startled to find Mozart turning operatic tradition upside down. Not only does Susanna have the most notes to sing, she is also the most interesting, quick-witted and lovable character in Mozart's rich portrait gallery.

Yet she is 'just' the chambermaid, one of whose most entrancing moments is her letter duet with the Countess, who dictates the words which are going to bring about the errant Count's downfall, while Susanna sweetly echoes them. It is a wonderful short scene in an opera filled with wonderful short scenes – and also with big, intricate finales, particularly that to Act Two, a *locus classicus* of comic pacing, brilliant resourcefulness and unstoppable verve, in which two groups of the principal singers verbally thrust and parry to achieve supremacy.

Here as elsewhere, the political aspects of the story – in which commoners score over aristocrats – make their point incisively. Figaro in his Act One aria *Se vuol ballare* ('If you want to dance') has already, in deliberately aristocratic minuet tempo, shown a ferocious contempt for his master quite the equal of the Count's own outburst of rage in Act Three. From beginning to end, tension intertwines with comedy, despair with élan, explosive jealousy with calm security in a wholly Mozartian way.

Though *Figaro* has been called a better-made opera than its successor, *Don Giovanni*, this does not necessarily make it the greater of the two. Each tackles its topics – sexuality, falsehood, aristocratic immorality, social class – in its own way. Each is an indispensable masterpiece. And each adds a new dimension to its literary sources. As the English publisher, Victor Gollancz, put it in one of his books of memoirs: 'Beaumarchais's *Figaro* is intrigue on earth; Mozart's *Figaro* is intrigue near the outskirts of Heaven'. For the proof of these words, you have only to turn to the last pages of the score, where the Count on bended knee asks the Countess's forgiveness, and the orchestra for a few moments holds us in the heights before bringing us back to reality in the closing chorus.

For the first performance of *Figaro*, Mozart assembled some sensationally youthful female singers. Nancy Storace, the original Susanna, was just 21; Luisa Laschi, the Countess, not much older; and Anna Gottlieb, the gardener's daughter whose poignant aria about the lost pin opens the final act, was merely 12. Today, in big international opera houses, these roles are usually portrayed by singers considerably more mature, and in world-class recordings the same tends to be true.

But unless you are determined to have singers of the renown of Elisabeth Schwarzkopf or Dietrich Fischer-Dieskau, there is much to be said for Sir John Eliot Gardiner's performance, one of the best of the more recent *Figaros* to be recorded. This has the forthright Bryn Terfel in the lead, but otherwise contents itself with light-voiced, less familiar, deftly integrated young singers, supported by the expert period instrumentalists of the English Baroque Soloists (DG Archiv 439 871-2).

Sir Charles Mackerras's is also very much an ensemble *Figaro*, with Alastair Miles admirable in the title role and Nuccia Focile as a Susanna with a refreshing touch of steel in her personality. Mackerras, who conducted a stylistically revelatory *Figaro* at Sadler's Wells in London in the 1960s, is in his element here, fascinatingly including more than half an hour of alternative versions of arias, and making the Scottish Chamber Orchestra play like a period band (Telarc CD 80388).

But if a great historic recording is to be your primary choice, look no further than the seductive Erich Kleiber version with the Vienna

Philharmonic. In 1955, when it was made, Lisa Della Casa's voice as the Countess was in full bloom. Hilde Gueden, as Susanna, may have needed a Mackerras to guide her stylistically, but she sang adorably all the same. As an added enticement, the set is now available at bargain price (Decca Legends 466 369-2).

Eleven

1786
PIANO CONCERTO IN C MAJOR, K503

Allegro maestoso   Andante   Allegretto

Of all Mozart's piano concertos, this is the biggest, grandest and most sonorous. Separating itself from the tragic manner of its immediate predecessor in C minor, it represents the C major summit of the 30-year-old composer's Viennese style. The two piano concertos that were still to come sound in comparison more like transitional works leading who knows where. All that can be said is that the so-called 'Coronation' concerto, K537, contains ornate and glittering foretastes of Chopin, and that the exquisitely frail, pure-toned B flat major concerto, K595, seems to suggest that, if this were not destined to be Mozart's last piano concerto, it would have marked the start of a new vein in his piano writing.

If the big C major concerto anticipates anybody, it is always believed to be Beethoven, particularly the Beethoven of the C major and the C minor piano concertos, which employ similar march rhythms, punchy chords and sharp contrasts between major and minor. Yet to play Mozart's concerto as if it were Beethoven would be a serious mistake. The music is Mozart through and through, in spite of its use (not for the first time) of martial trumpets and drums, and, in the first movement, blocks of chords rather than flowing lines.

Perhaps the grand ceremonial scale of the music has in some ways acted against its popularity. Eric Blom in the 1950s did his best to damage its cause by calling it 'frigid and unoriginal' – two wholly inappropriate words – in his then influential *Master Musician* study of the composer. Blom, in criticising it, at least had the courage of his convictions. What Wolfgang Hildesheimer, a more recent Mozart authority, thinks of it is something his excellent though quirky book denies us. Significantly or otherwise, he does not mention this great concerto at all. On the other hand, both Donald Francis Tovey, in a pioneering essay on the subject, and Charles Rosen, in a portion of his book, *The Classical Style,* have deemed the first movement worthy of the deepest, most appreciative analysis.

It is a masterpiece not only magisterial but also moving – broad and splendid, yet keenly detailed, in the first movement; touchingly chaste in the operatic sweetness of the slow movement, with its huge, expressive leaps in the solo part; and filled with gleams and shadows in the gavotte-like strains of the animated final rondo. Yet it is this finale which, for all its wit, is suddenly filled for a page or two with a wistful sense of life's fragile beauty and transitoriness — a feeling to be found in many other Mozart works, but never more intensely than in this 'ecstasy of joy and pain', as one commentator has perceptively put it.

The passage in question, once you have identified it, becomes a magical yet melancholy moment in every performance you hear. It is one of the greatest examples of Mozart's sublime simplicity. First, after some emphatic, anticipatory chords from the orchestra, the piano quite unemphatically plays a flowing phrase, repeated by the oboe-dominated woodwind. Then the piano extends the phrase, and the woodwind sustain the repetition. That is all. There is no more to it than that. The phrase never returns. But Mozart wrote nothing better, lovelier or more piercing in their combination of joy and sadness than these few bars. They confirm things that have been only hinted at earlier in the concerto – the tiny sighs amid the declamations of the first movement, the poignancy behind the descending phrases of the andante, evoking the nocturnal unease of the final garden scene in *Figaro*.

Yet this is not, on the whole, one of Mozart's more operatic concertos. It is as concerto-like as Beethoven's concertos, which is one reason why pianists are prone to perform it in a Beethovenian way. Such an approach is understandable. Even the predominant four-note rhythm of the first movement was to be employed by Beethoven in the first movement of his Piano Concerto No. 4. Moreover, and above all, it is the fundamental rhythm of his Symphony No. 5. Beethoven never concealed his admiration for Mozart's concertos, and in these two works – for those with ears to hear – he was surely paying public tribute to them. It is interesting that the second of them is in C minor.

Perhaps inevitably, good recordings of K503 are few and far between. Impersonal performances of it can indeed sound cold. The right 'tone' for the music, whether on a modern concert grand or on a Mozartian fortepiano, is elusive. But Alfred Brendel, not for the first time in his exploration of the handful of Mozart concertos he especially likes playing, gets it absolutely right. Happily, with Sir Charles Mackerras as conductor, the Scottish Chamber Orchestra – with an exhilarating sense of impulse at the start of the first movement – gets it right, too.

Brendel's virtues in this work include an unfailing sense of proportion and an unmistakable enthusiasm for the music. Enthusiasm, of course, is no guarantee of success; but Brendel's, which is controlled by mind as well as heart, is an enthusiasm of a special sort. To listen to his handling of Mozart's opening gambit – the piano makes its entry, slightly delayed, with something totally different from the expected reference to the main theme – is to know what true pianistic poise is all about. In the absence of a cadenza by Mozart himself, Brendel (as in his recording of the C minor Concerto) supplies his own model example, witty but never irrelevant. To the beauty of the slow movement he brings radiance and mystery, and in that short, magical passage in the finale he does not let us down.

The coupling, the so-called 'Jeunehomme' Piano Concerto in E flat major, K271 (whose nickname refers not to Mozart himself but to the name of the girl who originally performed it), is another work with which Brendel is deeply in love. With the piano making its entry as soon as the first page, it is one of a handful of early works in which Mozart's genius suddenly flared, as Brendel clearly underlines. The recording, made in the Usher Hall, Edinburgh, has a perfection of sound which has sometimes eluded Mackerras's technicians in his operatic recordings in the same surroundings, and which is all the more welcome here (Philips 470 287-2).

Composing symphonies came naturally to Mozart. The form was still young — it developed out of the early tripartite style of operatic overture, which in Italy was known as 'sinfonia' — and his first ones, mostly brief, were among the fruits of his Salzburg period and his boyhood travels. His last symphonies, altogether bigger and grander, were written when he was at the height of his powers in Vienna. By then he had brought what could be called the art of the symphony as he knew it to a state of structural perfection and extraordinary expressive range. Not even Haydn, traditionally hailed as the 'father of the symphony', and certainly the most inventive of all symphonists up to that time, surpassed him in these final works.

On the other hand, the bulk of Mozart's early symphonies supplied no evidence that masterpieces such as the 'Prague' or 'Jupiter' lay ahead. Most of them were the expert but superficial products of a busy boyhood, presided over by his father. Not until he reached Symphony No. 25, the 'little' G minor as it has been called in order to differentiate it from the great G minor Symphony No. 40, did it become clear that there might be more to Mozart the symphonist than seemed likely. By employing four horns, instead of the standard two, he suddenly achieved in this work a startling new sound-world, which was not 'little' at all.

By then he was 17 years old, and genius, though still elusive, was beginning to stir. Confirmation came in the beauty and poise of Symphony No. 29 the following year, and then, after a four-year gap, in the wit and élan of the 'Paris' symphony (No. 31). The compressed Symphony No. 32 brought new brilliance to the old-fashioned overture format. The punch of Nos 34 and 35 (the 'Haffner') and the grand maturity of No. 36 (the 'Linz'), which coincided with his escape from Salzburg, extended the map of his development.

But the fact remains that Mozart's great piano concertos, mostly dating from his Vienna years, were more numerous than his great symphonies, and haunt the listener in a different way. Given the choice between his symphonies and his piano concertos — the one body of inspiration against the other — it would surely not seem outrageous to opt for the concertos, even if it meant the loss of some masterly works.

Twelve

1787
SYMPHONY NO. 38 IN D MAJOR ('PRAGUE'), K504

Adagio – Allegro   Andante   Finale: Presto

Had Mozart, at the age of 25, moved from Salzburg to Prague rather than Vienna, what would have become of him? A similarly tantalising question could be asked about Beethoven, who seriously considered Paris as a place of residence rather than Vienna, but ended up in Vienna soon after Mozart's death. Either way, the history of nineteenth-century European music would have been altered, and Vienna's musical supremacy severely shaken, though more perhaps through Beethoven's absence from it than through Mozart's.

A Mozart living in Prague, after all, would not have differed radically from a Mozart living in Vienna. He knew both cities well, and received commissions from each of them. After its Vienna premiere, *Figaro* was an immediate hit in Prague. After its Prague premiere, *Don Giovanni* soon reached Vienna – and gained some fine extra music in doing so. Whether Mozart would have been healthier, wealthier and wiser as a citizen of

Prague is one of the unanswerable questions upon which all who deem his early death to have been the greatest of all musical tragedies are bound to dwell.

But *Don Giovanni* was not Prague's only Mozart coup. Nine months earlier, on 19 January 1787, the 'Prague' symphony had its premiere there, though it was actually composed in Vienna a few weeks earlier. Mozart's original plan had been simply to take a revision of his 'Paris' symphony with him, fitted out with a new finale. Once he had written that movement, however, he evidently decided that it was not enough. The rest of the old 'Paris' symphony was laid aside, two more movements were written in white heat, and the result was one of Mozart's supreme symphonic masterpieces.

Clearly he had recognised that his Prague invitation – the outcome of *Figaro*'s triumph in that city – was a big event in his life. He arrived there, complete with wife and sister-in-law, a week before the performance, which he directed himself to high acclaim. Thereafter he stayed on for a further three weeks, enjoying his celebrity and directing a performance of *Figaro*, concerning which he exclaimed that everyone 'was writing about it, talking about it, humming it, whistling it and dancing it'. Clearly this was why, after the premiere of the symphony, he had improvised twelve variations on Figaro's Act One aria, *Non più andrai*, on the piano as an encore. He also played, at a separate event, his latest piano concerto, the great C major, K503, which he had completed in Vienna two days before the symphony. Before leaving for home in February, he agreed to return in the autumn with *Don Giovanni*, of which not a note had yet been written and da Ponte had not yet been invited to write the libretto.

In the 'Prague' symphony, however, there were already foretastes of the opera. It was composed in the *Don Giovanni* key of D, and there was a conspicuous similarity between the ominous slow introduction to the first movement and the overture to the opera. But the most astounding feature of the symphony is the main body of the first movement, and the sheer scale on which it is structured. In no previous symphony had Mozart done anything like it, and only in the finale of the 'Jupiter' did he do it again. Its contrapuntal dexterity, rhythmic tension and melodic richness (the so-called 'second subject' is in fact the ninth melody to arrive in the allegro section) are protean, and inspiration is sustained throughout the rest of the work.

True, there is no minuet – which at one time prompted the Germans rather ponderously to nickname it the 'Symphony Without Minuet' – but that is because Mozart recognised that it did not need one. The quiet, seemingly calm but harmonically troubled slow movement, with its little sighs and sudden shadows, is all the more affecting because it leads straight into the sunshine of the finale, a movement whose circling momentum, with its cackling woodwind and pounding kettledrums, demands a conductor willing to accept Mozart's vital demand that each half of the movement be played twice.

Sir Charles Mackerras, in his recording with the Prague Chamber Orchestra, is one of the few conductors with the patience to do so – and it pays off in a performance of marvellous sweep, impulse and piquant colouring. The first movement, similarly extended, lasts more than sixteen minutes – as long, in other words, as the first movement of Mahler's Symphony No. 1. Yet the tension of the performance never slackens. The Prague orchestra, on this evidence, was not chosen merely for historic reasons, but because it can get inside the music and respond to a conductor who knows how to spice a modern performance with period features. With the 'Linz' symphony, finest of the predecessors of the 'Prague', as coupling, this is a disc so alluring that there seems little point in recommending any other (Telarc CD 80148).

If, on the other hand, you are one of those unfortunate people not to be on Mackerras's wavelength, then Christian Zacharias's performance with the Lausanne Chamber Orchestra would be an admirable alternative. It is cleverly coupled with the C major Piano Concerto, K503, in which Zacharias both plays and conducts, the way he did in his Mozart cycle at the Edinburgh Festival. Moreover, for good measure, Bernarda Fink gives a ravishing account of Mozart's greatest concert aria, *Ch'io mi scordi di te . . . Non temer, amato bene* (Dabringhaus und Grimm MDG340 0967 2).

Thirteen

1787
DON GIOVANNI, K527

Dramma giocoso in two acts to a libretto by Lorenzo da Ponte

Le nozze di Figaro ends with a night scene, full of false identities, misunderstandings, acrimonies and reconciliations. *Don Giovanni* begins with a night scene, in which similar but nastier things happen. Indeed, all its main events – the rape of Donna Anna, the murder of her father, the treacherous ball at Giovanni's house, the malicious serenading of Donna Elvira, the great sextet in which the cornered Giovanni turns out to be Leporello in disguise, the ghostly cemetery scene, the hellfire finale – are nocturnal. Mozart's supernatural key of D minor is hammered out in the two opening chords, and establishes itself throughout the slow introduction to the overture as the sombre, slithery, sulphurous obverse of brilliant D major, which is the opera's other main key.

Mozart accurately described *Don Giovanni* as a *dramma giocoso*, or 'jocular drama', rather than an *opera buffa* ('comic opera'). The latter, more familiar description would not have fitted a work in which the composer and his librettist, Lorenzo da Ponte, so audaciously mixed their genres. On the one hand, there were the formal and dramatic aspects, with their overtones of *opera seria*; on the other, there was the work's more harshly humorous side. The interplay between the two served to make *Don Giovanni* the arresting but problematic work it is. From the start, it invited criticism and created challenges; but the result was a masterpiece unique in operatic history up to that time, with Stravinsky's *Rake's Progress* (which was modelled on it) as its only great successor.

The abandoned but undaunted Donna Elvira, the domineering Donna Anna and her long-suffering suitor, Don Ottavio, are all self-consciously serious characters, even in the sort of music they sing – as the jerky mock-baroque rhythms of Elvira's *Ah fuggi il traditor* in Act One make plain. But the sardonic Giovanni and his scurrying servant Leporello run rings round them, and it is from this that the work's comic tension derives.

Mozart's portrait gallery is thereby rendered more human and more complex than the characters depicted in old-fashioned Handelian *opera seria*, and often more cruel than those in *opera buffa*. Leporello's famous catalogue aria, *Madamina*, in which he treats the lovesick Elvira to a list of Giovanni's amorous conquests ('in Spain a thousand and three'), is generally regarded as comic; but it can be made sadistically leering if the singer and stage director prefer it that way. Leporello, after all, is not only Giovanni's sidekick but also his would-be lookalike. Their relationship is quite different from that between Count Almaviva and Figaro in *Figaro*. Indeed, *Don Giovanni* as a whole is very different from *Figaro*, and different also from its successor, *Così fan tutte,* though they all have the same librettist, Lorenzo da Ponte, and various points in common.

In Prague, *Don Giovanni* had its premiere, after two postponements, at the National Theatre on 29 October 1787. The overture famously remained unwritten until the eve of the performance. It was an instant success, although (as has happened with many a modern opera, right down to *Sophie's Choice*) criticisms of the work would soon arise. The Mozarts had arrived from Vienna at the beginning of the month, and *Figaro*, with Mozart himself in charge, had filled one of the gaps left by the not-yet-ready *Don Giovanni*. When the new work was eventually unveiled, the audience clearly understood that it was no mere follow-up to a previous hit, but something even more ambitious and harmonically daring, and they loved Mozart all the more for it.

The revised version presented in Vienna the following year, which some people sourly took to be another of Mozart's attacks on the aristocracy, went down less well. Yet it received more performances than *Figaro* had done, and outside Austria it succeeded, particularly in France and Germany, where before long it was perceived to contain portents of nineteenth-century romanticism. With the enthusiastic support of E. T. A. Hoffmann, it became the Mozart opera with which audiences most closely identified – though today, perhaps temporarily, that position is held by *Così fan tutte*.

Of all Mozart's works, it is certainly the most Gothic and the one which is driven most powerfully to its close. Though what is regarded as its subtitle, *Il dissoluto punito* ('The Libertine Punished'), is actually its true title, nobody ever thinks of *Don Giovanni* as being a mere subtitle. It is not, in any case, primarily for being a libertine that the opera's anti-hero meets his fate. It is because he arrogantly invites the statue of Donna Anna's father, whom he has killed, to supper. Once he has done this, his fate is sealed. Yet the arrival of the 'stone guest', with its ice-cold handshake, does nothing to reduce Giovanni's defiance. Musically, with its braying trombones, this remains the most dramatic moment in all opera – if, that is, it is done well enough, which means well enough sung, well enough conducted, well enough presented, at the climax of a good enough performance.

Gustav Mahler, conducting *Don Giovanni* at the Vienna State Opera, ended the opera abruptly with this scene, thereby denying his audience the dazed return of the other characters and the final daylight pointing of the moral. It was a cut which, given the opportunity, some conductors and stage directors might still be willing to make, and which some audiences, by their premature applause, seem to expect. Vandalising *Don Giovanni* has become a heavy industry, from the monumental tableaux and slow scene-changes of Zeffirelli's overcrowded Covent Garden production, repeated in various forms around the world, to the crudities of Graham Vick's version for Scottish Opera (the so-called 'lavatorial' *Don Giovanni*, in which the champagne aria was sung in the loo), though much of it was acutely observant and funny.

But it is a work which responds more readily to variety of approach than *Figaro*, which is a more homogeneous but, in spite of its political and amorous overtones, less shocking masterpiece. Of the two works, *Figaro* is unquestionably the more lovable, but *Don Giovanni* – dare one say it? – the more compelling as a study of music as drama. The range of ways in which the protagonist himself can be portrayed – from the sleazy, balding, lecherous Giovanni sung by Renato Capecchi in a controversial but revelatory production at the Holland Festival in 1965 to all the sadists, spivs and dishonourable public schoolboys who have enacted the role since then – seems endless.

On disc, we need a performance which is not only finely sung and conducted but which also has some sense of operatic presence. Sir Charles Mackerras's recording, made at the 1995 Edinburgh Festival, has the virtue of speed, drama, stylistic integrity and musical comprehensiveness – both the Prague and Vienna versions of the score are incorporated, in such a way that listeners can make their own adjustments to the performance, depending on which version they wish to hear. Though the Usher Hall, where it was recorded, has its acoustical shortcomings, the atmosphere of the performance survives. The singers, even if not always heard to full advantage, sound like a real ensemble, with Bo Skovhus a racy Don, Catherine Brewer an edgy Anna, and Felicity Lott a far-from-limp Elvira (Telarc CD 80420).

It is a set, however, which faces stiff competition, not least from the fine Giulini recording, now more than forty years old. Conducted with unfailing beauty and intensity, this has Elisabeth Schwarzkopf's still-formidable Elvira as its primary asset, rather upstaging Joan Sutherland's droopy Anna. The male roles, topped by Eberhard Waechter, Giuseppe Taddei and Luigi Alva, are cast at strength, and the finesse of the Philharmonia Orchestra's accompaniments, like the performance as a whole, reflects the presence of Walter Legge as producer (EMI CD S5 56232-2).

Giulini's is a starry *Don Giovanni*, but Sir John Eliot Gardiner proves as usual that stars are unnecessary if the right young singers can be mustered to work with a conductor whose command of the score is total. With his own English Baroque Soloists, Gardiner states the case for a period *Don Giovanni* with powerful accomplishment; and the live recording, dating from 1994, has all the presence the music needs (DG Archiv 445 870-2).

Fourteen

1788
SYMPHONY NO. 41 IN C MAJOR ('JUPITER'), K551

Allegro vivace   Andante cantabile

Menuetto: Allegro   Molto allegro

C major is Mozart's Olympian key, nowhere more so than in the last and most dazzling of his symphonies, No. 41, traditionally known as the 'Jupiter'. Though the title was not Mozart's – the astute Johann Salomon, Haydn's London impresario, is said to have thought of it – it is thoroughly in keeping with a work which progresses from a seemingly simple, symmetrically classical starting point to a finale which is an unsurpassed example of sustained polyphonic panache.

During the summer of 1788, when he wrote it, all was not well with Mozart. For financial reasons, he had moved house to the Viennese suburbs, though he could still, as he said, afford a cab into town. Moreover, in spite of what he described as 'black thoughts' – the Mozart equivalent of Winston

Churchill's 'black dog' – inspiration was running high. The superb symphonic trilogy of which the 'Jupiter' forms the completion was written between June and August, though some of the music was probably already in his head, along with the sombre C minor Adagio and Fugue of the same period, and two of his best piano trios.

But if the use of conventional eighteenth-century odds and ends in the 'Jupiter' symphony – the first movement's opening call to attention, the four notes which launch the finale – suggests that it was composed in haste, what Mozart does with his ingredients sounds anything but hasty. Everything is fashioned with the utmost poise and with the most precise sense of timing. The way the first movement's opening phrase returns, after a mere twenty bars, in counterpoint with a chirpy woodwind overlay and a glowing horn insert is a sample of how classical formality in this symphony becomes witty and inspired. Even the use in the course of the first movement of what sounds like a captivating afterthought of a melody – it was written earlier that year for a baritone friend (the first Viennese Don Giovanni) to insert into another composer's opera – comes across as a stroke of genius.

Yet just because these three symphonies were written as a group, each of them in deliberate contrast with the two others, it is all too easy to treat them as the summit of Mozart's symphonic achievement. This, however, would be wrong. With Mozart, as with Haydn, each masterpiece from whatever period in his output demands to be taken on its own terms, as Mozart himself did. The Symphony No. 39 is not necessarily greater than No. 38 simply because it is one digit higher. Indeed, if we are to talk superlatives, there is a case for proclaiming No. 38 to be the greatest Mozart symphony of them all. And if we are to talk colour contrast, it belongs alongside the final three symphonies – transforming them into a quartet – rather than with its two predecessors, the 'Linz' and the 'Haffner', with which it is often said to form part of a set.

What can certainly be said is that the four last symphonies, from No. 38 onwards, fill a gap in Mozart's output left by his partial withdrawal from the writing of piano concertos. As someone who not only composed but performed and promoted his concertos in concerts devised by himself, Mozart had been finding himself to be one of fashion's victims. The Viennese public, as if awaiting the advent of Beethoven, had for the moment lost interest in Mozart's concertos.

Nevertheless, Mozart was by no means idle. Having composed the Symphony No. 38 for Prague, which had become his favourite of all cities, he set to work on his last three symphonies with no obvious destination for them in mind. They were composed, or so it would seem, for no other reason than that he wanted to compose them. No doubt he saw them as a form of security – evidence, for those who desired it, that he was not a spent force.

These symphonies, then, formed a sort of portfolio, akin to Bach's Brandenburg concertos. For No. 39, he chose the glow of E flat major, the future key of *The Magic Flute*, and gave prominence to the mellow sound of clarinets. From the euphony of this work, he moved to the passionate edginess of No. 40, written in his dark key of G minor, with stark and plaintive oboe tone replacing creamy clarinets (when he prepared an alternative version of this work for his clarinettist friend Anton Stadler, the result was not an improvement). Then, after the shadows of G minor, there came the high clarity of C major, in which every instrumental colour seems picked out against a white background. Here again there are no clarinets, and the tone of a single flute gleams like a halo above the oboes and bassoons.

After the classical wit and swagger of the first movement, the andante is a mysterious, atmospheric nocturne in which the strings are muted throughout. The mood is less calm than it promises to be. Even the silky opening theme is unexpectedly subject to disruption. As in other mature Mozart slow movements, we seem to be eavesdropping on some of the 'dark thoughts' to which he was prone around this time, and which keep breaking into the tenderness, delicacy and sweet woodwind lines of the music.

The minuet, too, has something jerky and unstable about it, with a stomping dance-beat which comes and goes, puncturing the suavity of the violin line. The central trio section, too, is disorientating, in that its opening passage is like a sentence in which the object comes before the subject. Or, to put it another way, it begins wittily with what sounds like a closing cadence, then adds the bars which should have preceded this. The joke, unusually, is all the better for repeating itself, before the music proceeds to the next section, based affirmatively on the four-note figure which, later, will serve as the finale's launching pad.

This final Molto allegro, after the repeat of the minuet, is quickly built into a contrapuntal juggling act, as more and more balls are tossed into the air and effortlessly rotated. The climax, where the contrapuntal tension is tightened to breaking point, sounds all the better if Mozart's repeat marks are fully observed, thus extending the acrobatics before resolution is finally reached. Alfred Brendel, who has admitted in his books to getting rather impatient with what he considers to be unnecessary repeats, has advised conductors against including these ones. But to drop them – and most performances drop at least one of them – is to miss half the movement's exhilaratingly relentless verve.

Sir Charles Mackerras makes no such omission in his recording with the Prague Chamber Orchestra, an outfit which, on this evidence, has great personality. Or is the personality Sir Charles's? At any rate, here is a 'Jupiter' as complete as can be – even at Mackerras's speeds it lasts as long as Beethoven's Seventh Symphony – with a similarly comprehensive account of the Symphony No. 40, in its superior oboe version, as coupling. But the conductor's vitality ensures that the music never dallies. This is a fitting continuation of Mackerras's recording of the 'Prague' and 'Linz' symphonies, and thus an automatic first choice among the multiplicity of recordings of these works. Articulation, once again, is stylishly 'clipped', yet the sound is full and bright and the performances fiery (Telarc CD 80139).

Fifteen

1789
COSÌ FAN TUTTE, K588

Opera buffa in two acts to a libretto by Lorenzo da Ponte

After the hit parade of *Le nozze di Figaro* and *Don Giovanni*, Mozart and Lorenzo da Ponte, the most gifted of his librettists, collaborated on one more human comedy, the intimate and increasingly disturbing *Così fan tutte* ('That's what women do'). For the completion of their operatic triptych, they approached the battle of the sexes from a different and what was long thought to be more superficial angle.

The libretto, originally devised for Salieri, was taken up by Mozart after his distinguished Viennese rival had discarded it. Both Beethoven and Wagner famously despised the resultant opera, Beethoven because he considered the story to be immoral and shockingly unworthy of Mozart's music. Wagner, going even further, declared with evident satisfaction that the deplorable plot had reduced the composer's inspiration to its own low level. Yet it is easy to see why Mozart was attracted to its sexual possibilities and its Viennese sophistication, even if his reasons for writing it remained personal.

By New Year's Eve 1789, at any rate, it was being rehearsed in Haydn's presence at Mozart's house, and by 21 January 1790, again in Haydn's presence, at the Vienna Burgtheater, where its premiere took place five days later. The commission, it seems, had followed a successful Viennese revival of *Figaro*, which received twenty-six performances in 1789. Though *Così fan tutte* initially scored only ten, that was partly because the death of the Emperor Joseph II on 20 February 1790 caused a break in its run of performances. Whether Mozart received the substantially increased fee he had been promised remains uncertain, but the work was undoubtedly a box-office success, attracting a fashionable public. Even if Mozart's popularity as a composer of piano concertos was by then on the wane, his standing as an opera-composer was continuing to grow.

In spite of nineteenth-century criticism of its artificiality, many people today place *Così fan tutte* at the pinnacle of Mozart's achievement, its message more in tune with the times, and far more penetratingly delivered than was formerly thought. Not for nothing was the Act One trio, *Soave sia il vento* ('Softly sighs the wind'), incorporated as background to John Schlesinger's film about the tensions of modern domesticity, *Sunday Bloody Sunday*. This sweetly sad music, with its gently billowing accompaniment, suggestive of the Neapolitan breezes of its opening line, provides the first real hint that, thanks to Mozart, the seemingly light-hearted story will steadily deepen, and that the underhand masculine trick around which the action revolves will soon turn sour.

Fiordiligi and Dorabella, the two sisters whose fidelity to their betrothed is to be put to the test, here voice their despair that their beloved Ferrando and Guglielmo have been sent off to war. What they do not realise is that it is all just a joke. The men, prompted by the scheming Don Alfonso, will return in disguise and woo each other's fiancée. If they fail in this endeavour, which is what they hope and expect, they will win the cynical Alfonso's wager.

But the ardour with which they assume their false identities ensures that the sisters are duped (in Victorian times the story was bowdlerised to make it seem that the girls secretly knew the truth all along). The disguises, though often considered a serious flaw in an otherwise realistic plot, perhaps suggest that the girls did not know their partners as well as they thought. At any rate, Don Alfonso wins his bet, and everyone ends up sadder and wiser, but ultimately reconciled. The moral, delivered in the closing ensemble, is sometimes deliberately obscured by modern directors in search of a different sort of truthfulness. It is, however, fully in keeping with the work's eighteenth-century philosophy.

Even when, according to Mozart's original intentions, the outcome softens the sexual issues set up by the story, *Così fan tutte* is a sharply observant comedy. Mozart himself, it may seem relevant to remember, loved one of two singing sisters (Aloysia Weber) then happily married the other (Constanze), and took both of them with him to Prague in 1787. Yet the opera's ending, even when allowed to preserve its original comic spirit, does not make the Act One trio, and other passages of its kind, any less emotionally truthful. The anguish of the girls, as they wave farewell to their future spouses, will soon be swept aside by other, more pressing, priorities. But it is genuine enough at the time, and Don Alfonso's mock sympathy for their plight, and mock prayer for the safety of their beloveds, makes their music all the more touching, and his words all the more cruel.

If *Così fan tutte* is a work which now seems to mean more than Mozart and da Ponte intended, this is surely because a reaction has taken place against productions which traditionally treated the characters merely as amusing marionettes, the whole work a joke less bitter than we have come to think. Tired of the farcical sight-gags which cluttered so many performances of *Così*, directors went to the other extreme and began to deny that there was anything funny about the work at all. Instead of sunny seascapes as décor, there were funereal cypresses. Instead of being reunited at the end, the two pairs of lovers would furiously refuse to meet each other's eyes.

So what is the truth about *Così*? The problem, for it has become a problem, lies in the beauty and ambiguity of Mozart's music, its heightened expressiveness as the bet begins to take effect. When, at the climax of Act Two, Ferrando successfully breaks through the defences of his friend Guglielmo's faithful Fiordiligi, an eloquent oboe solo – surely the most potent moment in the entire opera, and equal to anything in the great B flat major Wind Serenade – tells us that something more than a joke is at stake. Then when Guglielmo, during the mock wedding ceremony devised by Don Alfonso, breaks away from the others to say he hopes they are all drinking poison, he is not joking either.

When Scottish Opera first staged *Così* in Anthony Besch's perceptive and famous 1960s production, Janet Baker, who sang Dorabella, said in an interview with the writer of this book that she had become more and more aware as she got into the role that both men loved Fiordiligi, the more dominant of the sisters. It was an interesting personal response to the work's interplay of character, and it supplied one more link in the chain of ambiguities that sustain this most ambiguous of operas.

Yet, as Charles Rosen has pointed out in his book, *The Classical Style*, the irony of *Così* depends on its 'tact' – which is not, one feels inclined to add, a feature of this opera much in evidence today. There is, Rosen declares, simply no way of knowing in what proportions mockery and sympathy are blended in Mozart's music and how seriously he took his puppets. Why should Fiordiligi's big Act One aria, with its great vocal leaps and its martial pair of trumpets in the background, be an outrageously comic send-up of *opera seria*, whereas her big Act Two aria, with similar leaps and a pair of romantic horns, is genuinely serious and touching? All we can do is let the music speak to us in its own way. If it speaks ambiguously, that is what makes it so fascinating.

A good recording of *Così fan tutte* can be said to have the advantage of not distracting you from what the music is about. If it is a recording of a stage production, it may even seem to contradict what was seen in the opera house. Sir Charles Mackerras's recording with the Scottish Chamber Orchestra, being based on a concert performance at the 1993 Edinburgh Festival, is in no way at odds with what was presented on the platform, and has all the benefits of his other Mozart opera sets – expert pacing, keen ensemble and a fine sense of eighteenth-century style, all the more impressive because it is drawn from what is not fundamentally a period orchestra (Telarc CD 80360).

Janet Baker's revelatory Dorabella, a role she learned for Scottish Opera, can be heard alongside Montserrat Caballé's similarly penetrating performance in Sir Colin Davis's beautiful and sympathetic Covent Garden recording (Philips 422 542-2). Elisabeth Schwarzkopf and Christa Ludwig add lustre to Karl Boehm's sumptuously big-scale, conspicuously romantic 1962 recording with the Philharmonia Orchestra from the Walter Legge era, now at bargain price (EMI CMS7 69330-2). For intimacy, lightness of touch and sweetness of tone, however, the René Jacobs recording with Veronique Gens and Bernarda Fink as the sisters, and with the period instruments of Concerto Köln, is in a class of its own (Harmonia Mundi HMC 951663/5).

Sixteen

1790
STRING QUINTET IN D MAJOR, K593

Larghetto – Allegro	Adagio
Menuetto: Allegretto	Allegro

In his four last string quintets – a group of works claimed by some authorities to be not only Mozart's supreme masterpieces but to represent the art of music in its highest form – the composer added a second viola to the traditional eighteenth-century quartet ensemble of two violins, viola and cello.

There was no established precedent for doing so. Boccherini, thirteen years Mozart's senior, had generally preferred to include an extra cello in his vast and pioneering array of string quintets, principally because he was a cellist himself. Schubert, in his great C major Quintet of 1828, similarly used the deeper-toned instrument as ballast. But Mozart's choice, we can guess, lay in the fact that, when he was not playing the piano, the viola had become his favoured instrument. It was what he liked to play when he took part in performances of chamber music — on one famous occasion with Haydn, no less, as violinist. And he found that, in writing string quintets, the inclusion of two violas as middle voices gave him a balance of forces, with a central grainy richness of tone, which suited his tastes.

Apart from an early work in B flat major, and an inspired transcription of his C minor Wind Serenade, all Mozart's string quintets date from the last few years of his life, during which he was at work on his last three operas, his last three symphonies, his last three concertos, a variety of chamber music including a glorious string trio, and his unfinished Requiem.

These years, comparable with the equivalent period in young Schubert's career, were ones in which Mozart became increasingly concerned with death. His close friend and fellow-freemason, August von Hatsfeld, had died in 1787 at the age of 31; and, in his last letter to his father (who himself died around the same time), Mozart stated that he had come to make it his habit to imagine the worst in all situations: 'As Death, if we come to think about it soberly, is the true and ultimate purpose of our life, I have over the last several years formed such a knowing relationship with this true and best friend of humankind that his image holds nothing terrifying for me any more; instead it holds much that is soothing and consoling!'

If it is the resigned, veiled, valedictory beauty of the G minor Quintet, K516, which is particularly brought to mind by these words, we should not therefore think it a greater, deeper work than the less brooding D major Quintet which followed. But though, as Mozart remarked in the same letter to his father, 'I never lie down at night without thinking that perhaps, as young as I am, I will not live to see another day', he added that 'No one who knows me can say that I am morose or dejected in company'. It is Mozart's ability to present one face to the world, without entirely concealing his other face, that makes the D major Quintet the masterly, often ambiguous work it is. The G minor Quintet delivers its message with disturbing directness; the D major does it obliquely.

Yet the message is unmistakably there, contained in a single spread-out chord delivered by the cello towards the end of the slow introduction to the first movement. Before this moment of shock is reached, the cellist has played five other chords, each based on a different note and each answered with sweet poignancy by the other players. But the effect of the sixth chord, an eloquent, unexpected diminished seventh in a context of harmonic normality, casts a chilling shadow across the music which the D major brightness of the succeeding allegro does not wholly sweep aside.

Indeed, the coursing energy and bouncing rhythms of the main body of the movement – 'no one can say I am dejected in company' – do not lack secret shadows of their own. So, when the slow introduction returns near the end, with new modulations and more intense replies, it may not therefore seem wholly a surprise. Yet a surprise, and a masterstroke, is what it is meant to be. Mozart had never structured an opening movement in this way before. Thereafter its fast, robust coda should fool nobody.

The swaying, touching, pulsating slow movement – a real Mozart adagio rather than an andante – in any case takes us back to the atmosphere of the first movement's introduction, and to the slow movement of the G minor Quintet, whose exploration of rapt string sonorities it expressively extends. The minuet is firmly shaped and rich in tone, its central trio section more fragile, very pretty, with high arpeggios.

At the start of the 6/8 finale, the players are offered an interesting choice. Is the main theme to be performed as a swiftly descending, eight-note chromatic scale, as Mozart originally intended, or as the technically easier zigzag figure which mysteriously replaces it in print and was probably the work of Mozart's publisher? Either way – though Mozart's way is predictably better – the movement is a miracle of contrapuntal inspiration, sunlit but not unclouded.

The most desirable recording of this work is the one which has that most civilised of violinists, Arthur Grumiaux, as leader of a hand-picked ensemble of players. The death of this gifted Belgian in 1986 at the age of 65 was a sad loss, and all his recordings, including a superlative account of Bach's sonatas and partitas for solo violin, are to be treasured. Mozart's D major Quintet forms part of a complete three-disc set of these works, dating from 1973 and now available at bargain price. It is a performance whose truthfulness extends to the use of Mozart's own notes in the main theme of the finale.

(The quotations from Mozart's letter to his father are from Robert Spaethling's translation of Mozart's correspondence, published by Faber in 2000.)

Seventeen

1791
PIANO CONCERTO IN B FLAT MAJOR, K595

Allegro   Larghetto   Allegro

'Everything is cold for me – ice cold', wrote Mozart at the start of what was to be the last year of his life. He was not referring to the Viennese weather. His fame as Europe's finest pianist-composer, who had brought the art of the piano concerto to its zenith, was dwindling. He had cash-flow problems, though these were in the process of being resolved. He was suffering from depression. But, as Maynard Solomon has said in his magisterial Mozart biography, he 'somehow managed to stem the drift into silence'. He did so with a chain of masterpieces whose sheer quantity and variety – from *The Magic Flute* to the most subtle sequences of ballroom dances – he had not previously surpassed.

At the beginning of January, he completed the last of his piano concertos, K595 in B flat major. His clarinet concerto, his last great string quintet, his last two operas and a group of haunting miniatures – the *Little German*

Cantata, the funereal *Ave Verum Corpus* motet, the *Fantasia and Andante* for mechanical organ, the last few songs – still lay ahead, as also did the great unfinished Requiem. Though the last piano concerto has been thought to possess the quality of a 'transfigured farewell' – a very apt phrase with which to describe it – there is not the slightest evidence that Mozart himself thought about it that way, or that when he wrote it he was more than usually aware of his own impending demise. Those who say the music contains intimations of Mozart's death are merely being wise after the event. His death-consciousness applied to all humanity.

Yet after the glitter of the ceremonial 'Coronation' concerto, written three years previously, there is undoubtedly something very pared-down about K595, something deliberately pale about its colouring, something conspicuously inward-looking about its mood. Its orchestration, with just a single flute, two oboes, two bassoons, two horns and strings, but no clarinets and certainly no trumpets and drums, is almost minimalist by Mozart's standards at the time. Even the movement headings – 'allegro', 'larghetto', 'allegro' – are reduced to single words. All this seems significant; but whether it signifies death or what might have been the start of a new phase in Mozart's output of concertos is another matter.

Whatever else he had in mind – and it looked like quite a lot – further piano concertos at that point looked unlikely. When he played K595 on 4 March 1791, it was destined to be his last public appearance as a pianist before his death nine months later. The person who made this appearance possible was an old acquaintance – the successful clarinettist Joseph Baehr – who slotted it into a concert in which Mozart was quite clearly not the star. The programme, given in the hall of a restaurant-owner round the corner from Mozart's apartment, featured Baehr himself as the main attraction. Next in importance was the singer Aloysia Lange, Mozart's sister-in-law, whom he had loved and once hoped to marry. The information that 'Herr Kapellmeister Mozart will play a concerto on the fortepiano' came third in line.

Did the work's murmuring, walking-paced opening – an uncanny fore-taste of Schubert, who was not yet born – make its mark? Was the delayed entry of the first theme recognised as a subtle masterstroke? Were the downward scales and chromaticisms thought to possess a forlorn, wraithlike eloquence? Was the flow of the music, in which one theme merges with the next, perceived to be beautifully sustained, or did the audience fail to grasp such extraordinary continuity of line? Mozart's own cadenza, written into the score, adds to the first movement's special unity, as does the similarly personal cadenza in the finale.

The simplicity of the slow movement, which one distinguished but sometimes imperceptive authority on Mozart's concertos has deemed to be a sign of waning inspiration, is perfectly in keeping with the understated inspiration, and the veiled melancholy, of the rest of the work. Even the buoyant main theme of the rondo finale, which in an earlier concerto might have sounded like a vigorous hunting motif, has a delicate poignancy appropriate to the intimacy of the music. It is no surprise that Mozart employed almost the same melody in one of his last songs, entitled *Sehnsucht nach dem Frühling* ('Longing for Spring').

Though it might seem sentimental to point out that 1791 was to be Mozart's last spring, the sweet sadness of the music makes the temptation irresistible. Yet there is also a lightweight muscularity about this movement which makes it possible to draw quite different conclusions about its meaning. In his last piano concerto, as in so many of its great predecessors, ambiguity reigned supreme.

Among many fine recordings of this work, three in particular catch its fine-spun luminosity to perfection. Of these, the newest is Alfred Brendel's with the Scottish Chamber Orchestra under Sir Charles Mackerras – one of a series of Mozart recordings they have been making together. By shunning daintiness, yet preserving delicacy of touch, Brendel makes the music sound as strong as platinum. The coupling – splendid contrast – is the big E flat major Piano Concerto, K482, in which the SCO's wind instruments, piercing the orchestra's small string section, make the music sound at times like one of Mozart's great wind serenades (Philips 468 367-2).

Pure simplicity of utterance, of a sort which must have been hard to achieve, is the virtue of Emil Gilels's recording with the Vienna Philharmonic under Karl Boehm. The more jovial E flat major Concerto for Two Pianos, K365, in which the Russian pianist is joined by his daughter

Elena, adds to the disc's desirability (DG 419 059-2). If this is a classic recording, so is Sir Clifford Curzon's with the English Chamber Orchestra under Benjamin Britten — another performance in which the music is stripped to its essence, with the drama of the D minor Piano Concerto, K466, as a powerful obverse (Decca 417 288-2).

Eighteen

1791
THE MAGIC FLUTE, K620

Singspiel in two acts to a libretto by Emanuel Schikaneder

From a series of Italian texts, Mozart turned for his final opera to a German one. *Die Zauberflöte* is a vernacular comedy or *Singspiel* ('sung play') with lofty overtones which make it the source of Wagner as well as one of the foundation stones of German-language opera. It mingles music with spoken dialogue and is based on an oriental fairy-tale with words by Emanuel Schikaneder, an adroit actor and playwright who ran his own company in a Viennese suburban theatre and who himself played the comic role of Papageno in the opera's first production.

Like Mozart, Schikaneder was a freemason, and with the composer's encouragement he added a powerful masonic undertow to the plot, which fits oddly with the comedy yet adds to the musical stature of the work as a whole. The result, hastily written though it was and full of what look like loose ends, hangs together with its own strange coherence. Mozart mixed his genres here as challengingly as he had already done in his very different *Don Giovanni*. It is an opera which has been loved from the start and, had he not died too soon to reap its harvest, might have made him the fortune for which he lived in hope.

Like *Così fan tutte*, it has been accused of triviality, partly through its use of popular Viennese idioms of the period. Papageno's ditties sound like eighteenth-century pop songs, which just happen to have been composed by Mozart. On the other hand, the music of Sarastro the high priest could have come, as one critic declared, from the voice of God. The work's ideals rise above what was thought to be the shallow cynicism of *Così*, and Sarastro and his priests put Tamino and Pamina through various intimidating masonic tests and rituals before they can marry.

Yet the looming presence of Sarastro is undoubtedly the work's major stumbling block. Initially made to seem, by a trick of the plot, to be an evil ogre, he turns out to be a force for good. So why, before the curtain rises, has he kidnapped Pamina? Why has her mother, the seemingly caring and well-intentioned Queen of Night, hired Tamino to rescue her? Why is the sinister and manic Monostatos, who wants to rape her, a member of Sarastro's staff? Why does Sarastro sentence him to be beaten on the soles of his feet? Why, in a word, is Sarastro so macho?

At one time, it was thought that Mozart and Schikaneder had not properly worked out their ideas in their rush to get *The Magic Flute* performed. Then it was thought that they were introducing surprises — a

Sarastro who turned out to be good, a Queen of Night who turned out to be evil – in the manner of an unfolding detective story. And ambiguity, in any case, lies at the heart of Mozartian opera.

Yet today there remains something oddly disturbing about Sarastro and his priests, whatever they seemed like in Mozart's time. As Viennese masons in disguise, they evidently believed in the Enlightenment, as the sunlit ending of the opera symbolises. The trouble is that their methods now look too like those of a fascist dictatorship. Not for nothing did Peter Ebert's production at the Royal Scottish Academy of Music and Drama give them swastika-style armbands and get them to greet each other with 'Sieg-heils'. Not for nothing does Alfred Brendel, in his conversation book *The Veil of Order*, declare that he would like to get his hands on 'Sarastro and his mob' and bring harm to them in a way which Mozart did not envisage. But, whatever one's feelings about intervening in the plot of *The Magic Flute*, the work remains one of opera's milestones – lovable, tear-jerking in its simplicity, and seen at its best when staged fleetly and without elaborate staging. The bigger the theatre in which it is presented, and the more ambitious the décor, the more ponderously the action tends to move.

The titular flute, with its power to protect its player from physical harm, is traditionally wielded by Tamino while its strains emerge from the orchestra pit. Originally, however, it was genuinely played by Tamino himself, who in the first performance was Benedict Schack, a flautist as well as a singer. If it ever actually happened, it must have been a nice touch, akin to hearing Stravinsky's *Soldier's Tale* with a real violinist as the fiddling soldier (which this writer has experienced once in Edinburgh).

Though Mozart reputedly disliked the flute as an instrument, there is no convincing evidence of his distaste. His famous parenthesis on the subject in a letter to his father in 1778 is inconclusive. Concerning his tardy response to a commission for some flute music from a Dutchman called de Jean, he wrote: 'Moreover, you know that I become quite powerless whenever I am obliged to write for an instrument which I cannot bear.' The comment, examined and re-examined, has gone down in Mozart history. But the D major Flute Concerto, K314, one of the works he wrote, or arranged, for de Jean, is delightful, especially when James Galway plays it, even if it could hardly be called 'crucial' Mozart. Moreover, as a leading modern critic, Andrew Porter, has pointed out, the Eulenberg miniature score of the concerto translates Mozart's words quite differently as follows: 'And then, as you know, I am always "stuck" if I have to write all the time for one and the same instrument (which I dislike).'

Put this way, it seems uncertain whether Mozart was referring purely to the flute or to instruments in general. Porter's own, and neater, translation comes close to clinching the matter: 'Moreover, as you know, I always get fed up when – something I can't bear – I have to go on and on writing for the same instrument.' The issue remains unresolved. Robert Spaethling, in his fine American edition of Mozart's letters, does not side with Porter. Yet it would be nice, as Porter asserts, to be able to say that the composer of *The Magic Flute* did not dislike the flute. The music certainly suggests as much. The gentle flute lines, punctuated by softly syncopated percussion, which accompany the trials by fire and water, are the purest, most haunting music in the entire opera.

The fact that one of Mozart's sources was a popular work of the period entitled *Lulu, or the Magic Flute* was another, perhaps more obvious reason for his choice of instrument, deflecting him from the clarinet or basset horn, to both of which he was devoted at the time, especially for the masonic elements he detected in them. From its overture onwards, in fact, the work is very precisely orchestrated. Trombones, which had been voices of terror in *Don Giovanni,* revert in *The Magic Flute* to their more ecclesiastical origins, symbolising through their slow, sonorous chords in the opening bars the three knocks on the temple door which form part of masonic ritual. It is perhaps worth mentioning, however, that the short upbeats before two of the chords actually increase the quantity to five, representing, according to one authority, female masonry and thus the presence of women in Mozart's opera.

But three is the number which recurs obsessively throughout *The Magic Flute.* The cast-list includes Three Ladies, Three Boys, Three Priests and Three Slaves. The comical Papageno counts to three before attempting suicide because he fears he has lost Papagena, the girl he wants to marry. Even the basic key of the music, E flat major, has three flats as its signature. On the other hand, Pamina's Act Two lament, when she believes that

Tamino (undergoing a severely Orpheus-like test of his love) has lost interest in her, is couched in Mozart's darkly plaintive key of G minor, its anguished embellishments fully written out in confirmation of their importance, rather than left to the singer's discretion.

Striking the right balance between fun and solemnity in *The Magic Flute* is not easy, to judge by the number of performances that get it wrong. Tilt too far in one direction and it becomes moribund. Tilt too far in the other and it slides into tedious jokiness. On disc, the problem is less pronounced, though the large amount of spoken dialogue can become a bore if it is not pruned. Otto Klemperer's solution, which was to cut it entirely, seems much too ruthless. But his cast, with the shining-voiced Gundula Janowitz as Pamina, Walter Berry as a cosy Papageno, and Lucia Popp as a spitfire Queen of Night, are outstanding, the tempi less trudging than you might fear; and the Philharmonia Orchestra and Chorus, though their weight sounds Beethovenian, perform superbly. Even at bargain price, however, this is unlikely to be anybody but a canary-fancier's first choice (EMI CMS5 67388-2).

Among more recent conductors, Sir John Eliot Gardiner (DG 449 166-2), Sir Charles Mackerras (Telarc CD 80302) and William Christie (Erato 0630 12705-2) prove better weight-watchers. All of them favour brisk speeds, spirited singing, and the sound (or, in the case of Mackerras's Scottish Chamber Orchestra, the expert simulation) of a period orchestra. Gardiner's performance may be a bit too aggressive for some tastes, but an assertive *Magic Flute* is better than a placid one. Mackerras's may be as acoustically unfocused as his other Edinburgh opera recordings, but he gets the scale and spirit right and has, in Thomas Allen, the perfect Papageno.

But as an ensemble performance, even Mackerras's must yield to Christie's Parisian one with Les Arts Florissants, a recording ideal in its polished intimacy. Based on a production at the Aix-en-Provence Festival, it cannot, alas, convey the director Robert Carsen's revolutionary suggestion that the Queen of Night is not evil at all but is Sarastro's secret sidekick, operating on his behalf during the various trials through which the lovers are put, and sitting among the priests at their conferences.

As a concept, it made Sarastro a more plausible, if not necessarily more likeable, figure. Even without this gloss, however, the warmth, youthfulness and character of Christie's performance, with Rosa Mannion and Hans Peter Blochwitz as Pamina and Tamino, Natalie Dessay as the Queen of Night, Anton Scharinger as Papageno, and three excellent boys as the Three Boys, prove a constant pleasure (Erato 0630-127005-2).

Nineteen

1791
CLARINET CONCERTO IN A MAJOR, K622

Allegro   Adagio   Rondo: Allegro

The last months of Mozart's life seem uncommonly well documented by the musical standards of his time, yet the man himself can still elude us. Was he happy or unhappy, calm or disturbed, optimistic or pessimistic when he wrote this concerto, which proved to be his last instrumental work and last completed masterpiece? The music, as so often with Mozart, seems ambiguous, serene yet filled with undercurrents, nimble yet halting, sunny yet shadowy, depending on how you approach it. As the Mozart scholar Robbins Landon has asserted: 'No other work is more imbued with that final quiet resignation, but no other concerto has such a deep-seated satisfaction in pure orchestral sound.'

Though death was fast approaching, Mozart's letters at the time showed no awareness of it. To his wife, who was at a health resort taking the cure, he wrote of how he had eaten two 'delicious' slices of sturgeon and half a capon. He was sleeping well, had played two games of billiards, had sold his riding-horse ('that old nag') for fourteen ducats, and had sent his manservant to bring him black coffee while he enjoyed a 'marvellous' pipe of tobacco and orchestrated almost the whole of the finale of his Clarinet Concerto. That Mozart possessed a horse and a manservant may come as news to people who know only the famous stories about his poverty and his abject begging letters, which need to be taken with a pinch of salt. In 1791, it has been calculated, he was earning twice what a comfortably-off Viennese family needed to live on.

As for the success of his last opera, *The Magic Flute*, it clearly delighted him. It also filled him, as he put it, with 'a kind of urge' one night to play the glockenspiel in person, thereby upstaging his friend Emanuel Schikaneder in the role of Papageno. Schikaneder, the singing actor whose company was performing *The Magic Flute* at the Theater an der Wieden on the outskirts of Vienna, customarily played the glockenspiel himself while singing Papageno's Act Two aria, *Ein Mädchen oder Weibchen* ('A girl or a wife'). Inserting a glockenspiel arpeggio where none was written, Mozart startled the singer, 'who looked into the scenery and saw me there'. Replying in kind, Schikaneder inserted improvisations of his own in the aria's second verse.

More seriously, the composer reported the good impression the opera had made on his influential rival Salieri, who shouted his applause for every number. So much for the legend that Salieri was pathologically jealous of

Mozart's genius. Indeed, the self-confidence which Mozart expressed in his last letters suggests that his life was entering a new and more prosperous phase. His death soon afterwards was (to quote Landon again) 'surely the greatest tragedy in the history of music'.

But what, in this context, does his Clarinet Concerto say to us? Mozart's relish of the recently invented instrument – whose soft-edged yet penetrating tone he had loved ever since his teenage years – is apparent in every bar, yet the music's vivacity is shot through with what (admittedly wise after the event) we could call a vein of valedictory melancholy. Though this feeling is discernible in many of Mozart's earlier works, too, it is conspicuously intensified in the Clarinet Concerto and the B flat major Piano Concerto, K595, which are the two great concertos of his last year. But whereas the piano concerto contains the plaintive rasp of oboe tone as an ingredient of its orchestral accompaniment, the clarinet one confines the wind section to the more euphonious sound of flutes, bassoons and horns, achieving an effect whose warmth can make the music sound somehow all the sadder.

Significantly, the depths of the clarinet's register are exploited along with the heights – indeed, it was for a special, now obsolete, basset clarinet (an instrument akin to a basset horn with an extended downward compass) that Mozart composed this work for his gifted friend, Anton Stadler, after the premiere in Prague of *La clemenza di Tito*, in which Stadler had been a brilliant member of the orchestra. By then, Mozart was back in Vienna directing the first performances of *The Magic Flute*, a fact that underlines the frenetic activity of his final months.

But there is nothing frenetic about the concerto, whose central adagio – the inspired obverse of the larghetto of the equally great clarinet quintet – shows how it is possible to spin a mood of ineffably sweet sadness out of a bright major key. As for the faster movements that flank it, the first transforms smooth arpeggios into music similarly disconcerting, and the final lilting rondo has been summed up – once more by Robbins Landon – with a line from Shakespeare: 'Heart dances, but not for joy.'

Nobody can have performed Mozart's Clarinet Concerto more often than Jack Brymer, Sir Thomas Beecham's clarinettist in the Royal Philharmonic Orchestra, who continued his career long after the great conductor's death. Yet there is no hint of dull routine about the recording he made of it with Sir Neville Marriner and the Academy of St Martin in the Fields in 1973. The poignancy of the music is fully present beneath the surface grace and the swift sweetness of the finale. The coupling, Mozart's Oboe Concerto, K314, which also exists in a flute version, is an earlier, lesser work from the composer's Salzburg days, very charmingly played by Brymer's colleague, Neil Black (Philips 416 483-2PH).

But though this long-established recording remains unsurpassed in terms of tone quality and emotional perception, a more recent one by Thea King with the English Chamber Orchestra under Jeffrey Tate gets nearer the truth of the music in other ways. Instead of playing on a standard modern clarinet, she employs a basset clarinet modelled on the stretched version of the instrument built by the concerto's first exponent, Anton Stadler.

Stadler's perfected clarinet, with its conspicuously deeper register, failed to outlive him, just as the even deeper-toned basset horn, with which he was also closely associated and for which Mozart wrote with such eloquence, similarly became obsolete. But obsolete did not mean non-existent. Mozart's works requiring basset horns, particularly the great B flat major Wind Serenade, K361, and the Requiem, would be unthinkable without the softly rueful tone of these instruments. Likewise, the distinctive sound of the basset clarinet has returned, in a limited way, to the concert hall and recording studio as part of the modern authenticity movement.

Since Mozart's autograph manuscript of the Clarinet Concerto in its basset-clarinet version did not survive, Thea King has had to rely on a recent reconstruction of the original score. But the same, after all, has to be said about the standard performing version played by Jack Brymer, which Mozart himself had no hand in and which was not printed (with the lower notes altered) until after his death. The publishers, it is true, did this with sound commercial intentions, claiming that the work would be more widely performed if arranged for standard clarinet. The changes, nevertheless, should have been clearly marked.

What finally tips the scales in favour of King's disc, however, is not just the range of her instrument. It is also that it includes the similarly masterly

Clarinet Quintet, K581, in a parallel reconstruction of its basset-clarinet original. The two works, it has been been said, are like opposite faces of a single coin – and therefore inseparable. Thea King, with the Gabrieli Quartet, has given her performance of the concerto its perfect obverse (Hyperion CDA 66199).

Twenty

1791
REQUIEM IN D MINOR, K626

Introit	Kyrie	Dies irae	Tuba mirum	Rex tremendae
Recordare	Confutatis	Lacrimosa	Domine Jesu	Hostias
Sanctus	Benedictus	Agnus Dei		Lux aeterna

D minor was Mozart's most demonic key, the one he employed for the supernatural side of *Don Giovanni*, for the sulphurous first movement of his D minor Piano Concerto, K466, for the shadowy Kyrie, K341, and for the last of all his works, the unfinished Requiem, K626.

The story of how Mozart came to write it, and failed to complete it, is famous, though less mysterious than it has been made to seem. No vengeful Salieri – the man reputed (slanderously) to be Mozart's murderous Viennese enemy – lay behind the ominous nature of the commission, which reached Mozart via a supposedly sinister stranger in July 1791. The stranger, sinister or otherwise, was merely the lackey of a certain Count Walsegg-Stuppach, a would-be composer who commissioned music from other people and passed it off as his own.

Walsegg's wife having recently died, he wanted someone special to write a Requiem in her memory. Mozart was his man, but was extremely busy at the time, with two operas to finish by September and his Clarinet Concerto for Anton Stadler in October. Nevertheless, being always in need of ready cash, he accepted the commission (50 per cent in advance), though he delayed fulfilling it. This, no doubt, helped to account for the theory that the commission 'distressed' him and ultimately made him fear that he was writing his own Requiem. In fact, as the latest edition of the *New Grove* confirms, there is ample evidence to suggest that he was stimulated by the project, that Walsegg's identity was no secret (the count shared a villa with Mozart's close friend and benefactor Michael Puchberg), and that Anton Stadler was already earmarked to perform the major basset-horn part. What finally threw Mozart's knife-edge timing askew was the feverish illness which hit him in November, slowed his progress, brought him out in boils, and killed him at bar eight of the Lacrimosa. The theory that Salieri had poisoned him, given weight by Pushkin's poem on the subject and by Rimsky-Korsakov's opera *Mozart and Salieri*, was just one (though the worst) of the innumerable Mozart myths which continue to circulate about him. If anyone killed Mozart, it was more probably one of the doctors who bled him with inadequately sterilised instruments.

His death, at any rate, placed his widow in a quandary. Since Count Walsegg would have been unlikely to accept a half-finished work, Constanze Mozart expediently adopted the count's own tactics and got someone else

– the composer's pupil Franz Xaver Sussmayr – to complete it. Sussmayr, who had already been acting as the dying composer's amanuensis, did a resourceful job, using Mozart's surviving sketches and memories of discussions to fill out the unfinished music. Though the result was not authentic Mozart – how could it be? – it was unquestionably a musical entity, which has continued to this day to be successfully performed. Few if any members of the average audience would be aware of Sussmayr's plastic surgery on the music if they had not been informed of it beforehand.

Its mistakes and inconsistencies, however, have prompted more than one dissatisfied Mozart scholar to revise Sussmayr's efforts, usually to no avail. Among performers, loyalty to Sussmayr remains strong. One of the best and most recent of the interventionists, however, is Robert Levin, whose edition has been taken up in Britain by that most assiduous of Mozart conductors, Sir Charles Mackerras.

Conscious of structural inadequacies at key points in the Sussmayr original, and of easily adjustable infelicities of instrumentation and musical grammar, Levin has made many subtle alterations that can only be to the music's benefit. Of these, the most noticeable are the addition of a new and powerful Amen fugue (based on a Mozart sketch ignored or over-looked by Sussmayr) at the end of the Lacrimosa, the higher profile of the Hosanna fugue in the Sanctus, and the instrumental shadows which are atmospherically cast over the end of the Benedictus just before the short Hosanna reprise.

Yet the orchestration of the Requiem as it has come down to us has not been obscured. In fact, the reverse is true. Again and again, the sound has been meticulously cleaned up, corrected and purified. The burnished beauty of tone, brought about by the emphasis on basset horns and bassoons, alongside trumpets, pounding kettledrums and the uncanny timbre of an obbligato trombone in the Tuba mirum becomes intensified, and the deliberate absence of flutes, oboes and horns becomes even more noticeable.

The work as a whole shines forth as a final inspired combination of the traditional Austrian Roman Catholic side of Mozart's church music and his later devotion to freemasonry, complete with the very individual sound-world – here incorporating some touching hints of *The Magic Flute* – which he invented to portray it. In Robert Levin's revision, the Mozart–Sussmayr score is now surely as good as it is ever going to be.

Most recordings of Mozart's Requiem have drawbacks of one sort or another. Old-fashioned performances with big choirs and symphony orchestras no longer sound right for this work, whose stabbing rhythms and fierce dissonances have everything to gain from being performed by light-toned forces under a drama-conscious conductor.

For some years now, Sir John Eliot Gardiner's recording with the Monteverdi Choir and English Baroque Soloists has seemed the best in terms of scale and transparency of texture, its effect both intimate and powerful. Barbara Bonney, Anne Sofie von Otter, Hans Peter Blochwitz and Willard White are the high-calibre soloists, and the early D minor Kyrie, K341, forms a perfect pendant (Philips 420 197-2).

Fine though this is, however, it is now in danger of being ousted by Martin Pearlman's performance with the Boston Baroque Chorus and Orchestra, which has the great advantage of being the first recording to employ the Robert Levin edition. Though the soloists – Ruth Ziesak, Nancy Maultsby, Richard Croft and David Arnold – include no star names, this proves of no consequence. Pearlman's small forces, like Levin's edition, put the music under a microscope, and the result is a revelation. No fillers this time; but none is necessary (Telarc CD 80410).

As a fiercely dramatic experience, however, Sir Charles Mackerras's recording with the Scottish Chamber Chorus and Orchestra, issued in the spring of 2003, provides an even stronger case for the merits of the Levin edition. Susan Gritton heads the exemplary quartet of soloists (LINN CKD 211).

FURTHER READING

Peter Gay, *Mozart* (Phoenix, 1999; Penguin, 1999)

A short, fresh, neatly assembled American study, viewing the composer from various angles in chapters entitled 'The Prodigy', 'The Son', 'The Servant' and so forth.

Robert W. Gutman, *Mozart* (Secker & Warburg, 1999; Harcourt, 2000)

American blockbuster biography which covers, in more than 800 pages, the composer's cultural and historical background rather better than the man and his music. Though the style, like the book, is weighty, this is a study which usefully complements Maynard Solomon's.

Wolfgang Hildesheimer, *Mozart* (English translation, Dent, 1983; Farrar Strauss and Giroux, 1991)

A modern Mozart authority sets the record straight about many misconceptions. Required reading, belligerent and fascinating, sometimes irritating.

H. C. Robbins Landon, *Mozart's Last Year* (Thames & Hudson, 1988; Schirmer, 1990)

Almost all you need to know about the startlingly productive but ultimately harrowing final months of the composer's life, written by one of today's great Mozart experts.

H. C. Robbins Landon, *Mozart and Vienna* (Thames & Hudson, 1991; Schirmer, 1994)

The background to the composer's years as a freelance composer in the Austrian capital. Lively and picturesque, not too weighed down by scholarly detail.

William Mann, *The Operas of Mozart* (Cassell, 1977)

Big, juicy, blow-by-blow study of all Mozart's operas. Perceptive, immensely readable, sometimes quirky, written by the best, most virtuosic twentieth-century music critic of *The Times*.

Charles Rosen, *The Classical Style* (Faber, 1971; Norton, 1998)

A masterly, unsurpassed study of music in Vienna from Haydn to Beethoven, with Mozart at its heart. Needs a bit of musical knowledge, and preferably some ability to read music, but well worth the struggle.

Stanley Sadie (ed.), *Mozart and his Operas* (Macmillan, 2000)

Handy spin-off from the *New Grove Dictionary of Opera*, compiled by its industrious editor. Good, clear synopses and much other useful information, cleanly laid out.

Maynard Solomon, *Mozart* (Hutchinson, 1995; Perennial, 1996)

The one essential modern Mozart biography. Big, comprehensive, rivetingly written by a leading American scholar. Especially good on Mozart's finances, travels and relationship with his father.

Robert Spaethling, *Mozart's Letters, Mozart's Life* (Faber, 2000; Norton, 2000)

Vivid new translation of a generous selection of Mozart's letters written from all over Europe to his father and others. Less comprehensive than Emily Anderson's pioneering volume, but more attentive to the composer's very personal, often outrageous writing style. Biographical details usefully supplied by the American editor and translator himself.

GLOSSARY

Adagio. Italian musical term meaning 'slow', often interpreted as very slow.

Allegro. Italian musical term meaning 'light' or 'fast'. But is an 'allegretto' (meaning, literally, 'a little allegro') slower or faster than allegro? The term is usually accepted as meaning slower, but is irritatingly ambiguous.

Andante. Italian musical term meaning 'at walking pace'.

Andantino. Irritatingly ambiguous Italian musical term, usually taken to mean a little faster than andante, but which can also be interpreted as a little slower than andante.

Aria. Italian word for 'song' or 'air', performed by a solo singer, particularly in an operatic context.

Arpeggio. Split chord, i.e. a chord whose notes are spread in a harplike manner instead of being sounded simultaneously.

Assai. Italian word for 'very'.

Baritone. Low male voice, pitched between tenor and bass.

Basset clarinet. Clarinet with an extended lower register, invented by Mozart's friend, Anton Stadler, who employed it in his performances of the Clarinet Concerto, K622, and Clarinet Quintet, K581. Long obsolete; but modern versions of the instrument have been made for use by authenticity-conscious players.

Basset horn. Species of large, deep-toned clarinet, much loved by Mozart in his Vienna years, when he used it primarily for masonic purposes, but also in his big B flat Wind Serenade, K361, and his opera *La clemenza di Tito*.

Breeches role. Also known as trousers role. An operatic part in which a male character is played by a woman. The role of Cherubino in *Figaro's Wedding* was specifically written in such a way. But castrato roles, originally a feature of *opera seria* and devised for male singers whose pre-puberty voice had been preserved by castration, are also now performed by women in the manner of breeches roles. This is increasingly preferred to the only realistic alternative, which is to transpose the music downwards for tenor or baritone voice. Idamante in *Idomeneo* is such a role.

Cadenza. Solo passage of varying length, particularly in the first movement of a concerto or in a vocal work, enabling the soloist to display his/her technique in an improvisational manner relevant to the work being performed. Classical cadenzas traditionally end with a trill, serving as a signal to the conductor and orchestra to get ready to rejoin the soloist. Mozart wrote down some of his own cadenzas for concertos, providing invaluable information on how he performed such passages.

Canon. Put simply, a 'catch' or a 'round'. Piece of music, or section of a piece, in which a melody performed by one voice or instrument is repeated by one or more others, each entering before the previous voice has finished. As a result, the melody is presented in a constantly overlapping form. A double canon is an elaborate form of canon featuring two simultaneous canons for two voices each – also known as a 'canon four in two'.

Chromaticism. The use of chromatic chords or scales which, in piano terms, employ all the black notes as well as the white notes of the keyboard. Chromatic harmony is therefore richer than simple diatonic harmony, based on the notes of the normal major or minor scale.

Concerto. Work for solo instrument (or several instruments) and orchestra, usually in three movements. Mozart perfected the art of the piano concerto.

Counterpoint. The combination of two or more melodies or musical figures in such a way that they make musical sense.

Divertimento. A piece of entertainment music, usually for a group of instruments (strings and/or wind), in several movements.

Double bassoon. The lowest woodwind instrument regularly employed in an orchestra or ensemble. It has a compass an octave lower than a bassoon's. Rarely used before the nineteenth century; but Mozart included a part for it in his great Serenade for thirteen wind instruments.

Finale. The concluding movement of a work (e.g. symphony, string quartet, sonata) in several movements.

Gavotte. Antique dance-form, akin to a minuet, but with four beats in the bar instead of three. A tradition of the gavotte is that it begins on the third beat. Mozart, particularly in his early years, occasionally employed the rhythm of the gavotte as an ingredient of his concert music. Bach included gavottes in many of his dance suites, and Prokofiev's *Classical Symphony* contains a witty pastiche of a baroque gavotte.

K. Abbreviated prefix referring to the Köchel index of Mozart's works. Ludwig von Köchel (1800–77) was an Austrian scholar whose catalogue provides the standard chronological reference numbers for Mozart's works. Thus K216 is the index reference for the Violin Concerto in G major. The catalogue, largely accurate, has been subject to a degree of modern revision.

Konzertmeister. Concert master. Leader or director of an orchestra or ensemble.

Larghetto. Italian musical term meaning 'slow and dignified'.

Maestoso. Italian musical term meaning 'majestic'.

Mezzo-soprano. Female voice pitched halfway between soprano and contralto. Today the term (often abbreviated to 'mezzo') tends to be employed in preference to 'contralto', now almost obsolete.

Minuet. Dance in triple-time usually employed by Mozart as the second or third movement of a string quartet, or the third movement of a symphony. The contrasted middle section of a minuet is known as a trio, because there was a tradition of writing it in three-part harmony.

Moderato. Italian musical term meaning 'at moderate speed'.

Molto. Italian word for 'very'.

Non troppo. Italian musical term meaning 'not too much'.

Obbligato. Italian term employed when an instrument has a special 'obligatory' role in a piece of music, usually in conjunction with the human voice. Thus, in Mozart's case, an operatic aria may have a clarinet obbligato or a violin obbligato in addition to a general orchestral accompaniment.

Piano quartet. A work for piano with (usually) a trio of strings, consisting of violin, viola and cello.

Pizzicato. Plucked note on a string instrument.

Polyphony. Greek word meaning 'many voices', i.e. the simultaneous sounding of different lines, melodies or notes. Synonymous with counterpoint.

Presto. Italian musical term meaning 'fast', often taken to mean as fast as possible (which would in fact be *prestissimo*).

Rondeau. A rondo in the French manner. Term used by Mozart when writing in that style.

Rondo form. Italian term for what was traditionally the spirited finale of a symphony, string quartet or sonata. The word refers to the fact that the opening theme or section of the movement keeps recurring, or coming 'round' again, thereby forming an essential part of the music's structure. Slow movements can also be in rondo form.

Scherzo. Italian word for 'joke'. Title applied, particularly by Beethoven, to what until then had been a movement in the form of a minuet. Mozart wrote no scherzos, though Haydn occasionally used the term.

Sonata. A work consisting of three or four carefully structured movements. A three-movement Mozart sonata usually has a slow movement enclosed between two faster ones.

Sonata form. Term describing the structure of what was usually the first movement of a sonata during Mozart's period and later. Put simply, it consisted of an 'exposition', based on two or more contrasted themes, a 'development' section in which the material already heard is altered, developed, broken up or tautened in various ways, a 'recapitulation' in which the introductory material is assembled in something like its original form, and a 'coda' or tailpiece, which rounds the music off or brings it to some sort of closing climax.

Sonority. Sound. The sonority of a group of wind instruments is the sound they make when performing together.

Soprano. The highest female voice, ranging from middle C upwards.

Sostenuto. Italian musical term meaning 'sustained'.

String bass. Colloquial term for double bass, the lowest string instrument regularly employed in an orchestra or ensemble.

String quartet. A work for four string players, traditionally two violins, viola and cello. Haydn perfected the form, to which Mozart, Beethoven and Schubert all made major contributions. A string quartet is also an ensemble which performs string quartets.

String quintet. As above, but with an extra player, selected by the composer. Mozart's quintets had a second viola. Schubert, in his solitary string quintet, preferred two cellos.

Symphony. Form of orchestral work in several movements, usually of an ambitious nature. Much favoured by Haydn (known as the 'father of the symphony'), Mozart, Beethoven and Schubert.